Industrial Developmen
19

RICHARD  FALLIS,

# Industrial Development
## and
# Irish National Identity
## 1922–1939

## Mary E. Daly

SYRACUSE UNIVERSITY PRESS

First Edition 1992
92 93 94 95 96 97 98 99      6 5 4 3 2 1


The paper used in this publication meets the minimum requirements of American National Standard for Information Sciences—Permanence of Paper for Printed Library Materials, ANSI Z39.48–1984.∞™


**Library of Congress Cataloging-in-Publication Data**
Daly, Mary E.
    Industrial development and Irish national identity, 1922–1939
    Mary E. Daly.
        p.    cm.—(Irish studies)
    Includes bibliographical references and index.
    ISBN 0-8156-2561-8
    1. Industry and state—Ireland—History—20th century.
2. Ireland—Industries—History—20th century.   3. Ireland—Economic
conditions—1918–1949.   4. Nationalism—Ireland—History—20th
century.   I. Title   II. Series: Irish studies (Syracuse, N.Y.)
HD3616.I742D35    1992
338.09417—dc20
                                                            91-42446

*For Elizabeth*

MARY E. DALY is Statutory Lecturer in Modern Irish History at University College Dublin. She was educated at University College Dublin and Oxford University. She is a member of the Royal Irish Academy and joint editor of *Irish Economic and Social History*. Her publications include *A Social and Economic History of Ireland since 1800; Dublin: The Deposed Capital, A Social and Economic History, 1860–1914; The Famine in Ireland;* and *The Origin of Popular Literacy in Ireland: Language Change and Educational Development, 1700–1920* (coedited with David Dickson).

# Contents

# Tables

# Acknowledgments

THIS BOOK could not have been written without the co-operation of a number of individuals and institutions. I am particularly grateful to those who afforded me access to records that were not in public achives; the Department of Industry and Commerce, where Roddy Mulloy and Terry Lonergan provided invaluable assistance; the Department of Finance, where Colm Gallagher and Greg O Duill eased the research burden considerably; Liam Connellan and the staff of the Confederation of Irish Industry. I also wish to thank the staff at the National Archives, especially Anne Neary; Kerry Holland, Seamus Helferty, and everyone in the Archives Department of University College Dublin; Mary Clarke in the Dublin Corporation Archives; and the staff of the Manuscript Room in the National Library. Esther Semple and Tony Eklof of the Official Publications Section in the library of University College Dublin deserve my special thanks.

Dr. Jeremiah Dempsey told me about the early years of Irish Tanners; Conor, Lawrence, and Niall Crowley provided background material on their remarkable father, Vincent Crowley; Tom Barrington and his daughter Anne filled in details on their father and grandfather, J. Barrington, one of the most talented of Ireland's early public servants. Frank Casey, managing director of the Industrial Credit Company, provided printed and oral material on that organization.

This manuscript was completely rewritten while I was a Visiting Scholar at Harvard's Minda de Gunzburg Center for European Studies—an environment that gave me a much broader perspective on the modern Irish economy and brought me into contact with many people asking similar questions about different countries. I am

xii     *Acknowledgments*

profoundly grateful to CES for giving me two years' hospitality, most especially to Stanley Hoffman, Guido Goldman, and the indispensable Abbie Collins. Olwen Hufton proved a true friend throughout my time there, and Louise Richardson was a kindred Irish spirit. I also wish to thank Jim Cronin, Ronan Fanning, Peter Hall, David Jacobsen, Kieran Kennedy, Patrick Lynch, Dermot McAleese, Cormac O'Grada, Kevin O'Neill, and Kevin O'Rourke. My children, Paul, Elizabeth, Nicholas, and Alice, provided constant interruptions (four during the course of writing this acknowledgement) but help me to keep my sense of priorities. My greatest debt is to P.J. whose unrivaled knowledge of contemporary Irish industrial development has been a major influence on this book.

Monktown, County Dublin                                    Mary E. Daly
October 1991

# Abbreviations

THE INDEPENDENT IRISH STATE that came into existence following the Anglo-Irish treaty of 1921 was known as the Irish Free State, or Saorstat Eireann, until the name was changed to Ireland, or Eire, in the 1937 Constitution. In the interest of simplicity, the terms *Ireland* and *Irish* are used throughout.

In citing works in the text, short titles have generally been used. Frequent citations have been identified by the following abbreviations:

| | |
|---|---|
| ACC | Agricultural Credit Company |
| Agr. | Commission on Agriculture, Dail Eireann |
| BC | Banking Commission |
| BI | Bank of Ireland Archives |
| B Papers | Brennan Papers, National Library of Ireland |
| BT | Board of Trade, Public Record Office, London |
| Cab. | Cabinet Papers, Public Record Office, London |
| CBC | Currency, Banking, and Credit Commission of Inquiry |
| *C. Pop.* | *Census of Population* |
| *C. Prod.* | *Census of Production* |
| CVO | Commission on Vocational Organisation minutes, National Library of Ireland |
| DIDA | Dublin Industrial Development Association |
| DMA | Dublin Municipal Archives |

| ESB | Electricity Supply Board |
|---|---|
| F | Finance series, Department of Finance |
| FIC | Fiscal Inquiry Committee, Dail Eireann |
| FII | Federation of Irish Industries, Confederation of Irish Industry |
| FIM | Federation of Irish Manufacturers, Confederation of Irish Industry |
| ICC | Industrial Credit Company |
| IIDA | Irish Industrial Development Association |
| ILO | International Labour Organisation |
| Inds. | Inds. series, Industries files, Department of Industry and Commerce |
| Inds. A | Inds. A series, Industries files, Department of Industry and Commerce |
| Inds. B | Inds. B series, Industries files, Department of Industry and Commerce |
| *Ir. Ind. Yrbook.* | *Irish Industrial Yearbook* |
| *IT* | *Irish Times* |
| ITGWU | Irish Transport and General Workers Union |
| *ITJ* | *Irish Trade Journal and Statistical Bulletin* |
| ITUC | Irish Trade Union Congress |
| Lalor | James Fintan Lalor address, National Library of Ireland |
| McG Papers | McGilligan Papers, University College Dublin Archives |
| M.P. | Member of Parliament (England) |
| NAIDA | National Agricultural and Industrial Development Association |
| NLI | National Library of Ireland |
| NUBSO | National Union of Boot and Shoe Operatives |
| PDDE | Published Debates, Dail Eireann |
| PDSE | Published Debates, Seanad Eireann |
| PRO | Public Record Office, London |
| S | Supply series, Department of Finance |

T          T 160 series, Treasury Papers, Public Record Office, London
TC         Tariff Commission
T.D.       Teachta Dala (Member of the Dail, or Irish Parliament)
TID        Trade and Industries Division
TIM        Trade, Industry, and Mining

Industrial Development and Irish National Identity
1922–1939

# 1 The Irish Economic Desideratum

*Nineteenth-century Economic Decline*

THE NINETEENTH-CENTURY IRISH ECONOMY experienced considerable upheaval. In 1841 Ireland's population was over three times that of Scotland and more than half that of England and Wales; by 1921 Ireland contained 10% fewer people than Scotland and only one-ninth the population of England and Wales (Kennedy, Giblin, and McHugh 1988, 4). Ireland under the Union experienced the Great Famine of the 1840s, sustained emigration, population decline, and substantially less employment in manufacturing industry. In 1841 more than 27% of the labor force was engaged in manufacturing; fifty years later this had fallen to 17%, and more than two-thirds of this reduced work force was based in northeast Ulster. Both Dublin and Cork saw the manufacturing share of their work force halved between the famine and the early twentieth century, and many parts of Ireland were almost totally devoid of industrial employment. Agricultural employment also fell sharply due to the shift from labor-intensive tillage to cattle grazing, though overall living standards rose sharply, in part because of population decline. How far these events can be attributed to the Act of Union of 1800 is too broad an issue for discussion here. While Ireland's economic performance under the Union was not the sole factor fueling the movement for independence, it is hardly a coincidence that Ulster, the most successful province under the Union, rejected independence.

The economic failure of nineteenth-century Ireland was an issue

3

that gave rise to repeated comment. One detached observer, Friedrich Engels, attributed Ireland's poor performance to an absence of coal, which had been swept away millions of years earlier, condemning the country "as if by Nature's decree" to remain an agricultural nation (Mansergh 1965, 107). Few Irish nationalists accepted that interpretation. Books such as Sir Robert Kane's *Industrial Resources of Ireland* published in the year 1844 argued that Irish resources were more than sufficient to sustain a strong industrial nation, a message repeated by witnesses to the Select Committee on Industries (Ireland) of 1884–1885. Irish nationalists such as Young Irelander Thomas Davis and Sinn Fein's Arthur Griffith adopted this message uncritically (Davis 1989, 186; Davis 1974, 133), and it is not surprising that one of the earliest initiatives by Dail Eireann was the establishment of a Commission on Industrial Resources.

*The Political Factor in Irish Economics*

Denied the excuse of a lack of natural resources commentators were forced to seek an alternative explanation, and they found it in the political sphere. Horace Plunkett remarked that "the people have an extraordinary belief in political remedies for economic ills: and their political leaders, who are not as a rule themselves actively engaged in business life, tell the people, pointing to ruined mills and unused water power, that the country once had diversified industries, and that if they were allowed to apply their panacea, Ireland would quickly rebuild her political life" (Plunkett 1905, 33–34). The belief that the condition of the Irish economy was politically determined dated back to eighteenth century writers such as Jonathan Swift, George Berkeley, and John Hely Hutchinson. The apparent coincidence between industrial decline and loss of an Irish parliament encouraged an exaggerated belief in the power of politics to determine economic well-being, an interpretation given greater credence because the interventionist policies of the late eighteenth-century Irish parliament coincided with a period of prosperity. Dublin and Cork artisans in the early nineteenth century saw the re-establishment of an Irish parliament as the solution to unemployment and this vision persisted. Daniel O'Connell, the early-nineteenth century constitutional nationalist, advocated protection for Irish industry, and in the 1840s the Repeal Association produced a report that emphasized the benefits of tariffs. Young Ireland's Thomas Davis enthused about Germany's industrial development through tariff protection and claimed that given such measures and a native government Ireland could support a population of up to 35 million people (Davis, 1988, 186, 191–92). The debate on industrial decline and the efficacy of protection waned in the immediate post-famine years only to revive in the early 1880s—a period that saw the coincidence of commercial depression and a renewed campaign for self-government. In 1885, Charles Stewart Parnell expressed the belief that industrial revival would prove impossible unless Ireland had an elected parliament with tariff-creating powers (Lyons 1977, 296), and this message was reiterated by Sinn Fein's Arthur Griffith in the early years of the twentieth century when he cited, or rather misinterpreted, the German economist Friedrich List's infant industry thesis to justify his case. Griffith claimed that England had deliberately stifled Irish competition whereas an Irish parliament would have protected industry, leading to population increase at a rate similar to England's (Davis, 1974, 130).

The force of these arguments was bolstered by references to history. The publication of James Anthony Froude's *The English in Ireland* in 1872–1874 made the economic ideas of eighteenth-century writers known to a new generation and led to the reprinting of Hely Hutchinson's *The Commercial Restraints of Ireland.* This pamphlet emphasized the extent to which Irish economic development was determined by government legislation (Cullen 1969, 117). Subsequent historical writings, notably W. E. H. Lecky's *History of Ireland in the Eighteenth Century,* confirmed this interpretation as did later works such as Alice Effie Murray's *The Commercial Relations between Great Britain and Ireland* (1903) and the writings of George O'Brien. In his introduction to E. J. Riordan's *Modern Irish Trade and Industry,* O'Brien wrote, "The industrial decay of Ireland was caused therefore, by no failing of character either on the part of the employer or of the workmen, but was the result of the fiscal changes which were introduced at the Union and completed twenty years later" (1920, 50).

By the time of independence the case in favor of intervention, and specifically of protection, appeared to be well established among the ranks of the dominant Sinn Feiners. Voluntary efforts at industrial revival had been tried and found wanting. During the 1880s industrial exhibitions were held in Cork and Dublin, and efforts were made to establish a permanent body for industrial promotion. Dublin Corporation set up a committee to investigate industrial development, and the British Parliament was persuaded to establish a select committee on Irish industry. These efforts lapsed in the 1890s with the waning possibility of Home Rule but were renewed with the establishment in 1899 of an Irish Department of Agriculture and its publication of *Ireland Industrial and Agricultural*, an extensive handbook documenting Ireland's mineral, agricultural, and industrial resources, which was compiled for the Irish pavilion at the 1901 Glasgow International Exhibition (Coyne 1902, preface). It was initially intended that the Department of Agriculture should have responsibility for industry, but it was restricted to promoting rural handcrafts. Nevertheless the Irish pavilion in Glasgow sparked a new wave of exhibitions, the Cork Exhibition in 1902 and the Dublin International Exhibition of 1907, both organized with a view to promoting Irish industry. The Cork Exhibition resulted in the establishment of a permanent promotional body, the Cork Industrial Development Association, and ultimately in the emergence of a host of similar organizations, the largest being the Dublin Industrial Development Association, while the Irish Industrial Development Association was established to promote an Irish trademark. Many of those active in promoting Irish industry were supporters of Sinn Fein (Davis 1974, 132).

No commentator emerged, with the exception of James Connolly, to question the efficacy of government intervention. In 1910 in *Labour in Irish History* Connolly presented a Marxist analysis that argued that the fate of the Irish economy was determined by developments in international capitalism rather than by the presence or absence of a native parliament and its policies (1973, 28). However, in this as in other areas, Connolly's was an isolated voice. While Horace Plunkett rejected the simplistic nationalist version of Irish economic failings and pointed to the role of education and the values engendered by Catholicism, he incorporated the conventional analysis of the evils of British economic policy into his more sophisticated critique of the Irish economy.

The commercial restraints sapped the industrial instinct of the people—an evil which was intensified in the case of the Catholics by the working of the penal laws. When these legislative restrictions upon industry had been removed, the Irish, not being trained in industrial habits, were unable to adapt themselves to the altered conditions produced by the Industrial Revolution, as did the people in England. . . . It is not, therefore, the destruction of specific industries, or even the sweeping of our commerce from the seas, about which most complaint is now made. The real grievance lies in the fact that something had been taken from our industrial character which could not be remedied by the mere removal of the restrictions. (Plunkett 1905, 18–19)

### The Agrarian Interest

By 1900 the British and Irish economies were closely intertwined. Even before the Union Britain absorbed 85% of Irish exports and supplied 79% of imports (Cullen 1968, 45). The nineteenth century brought a common currency, integrated banking and transport, and a common Anglo-Irish market. While Griffith contemplated with equanimity a fundamental restructuring of the banks and stock exchange to assist an Irish industrial revival (Davis 1974, 134), the longstanding connections between the two economies could not be dismantled without pain. Enthusiasts for an industrialized protectionist Ireland failed to appreciate the strength of Anglo-Irish links. Irish agriculture was dominated by cattle farming, which had expanded to meet the needs of the British market as had industries such as shipbuilding, brewing, and biscuit making. Cattle farming and export industries provided a powerful lobby favoring the status quo though the farming community had more influence on nationalists than the predominantly unionist industrialists had.

Agriculture was frequently deemed to be in need of remedial assistance. Postfamine market conditions favored the expansion of cattle at the expense of tillage with consequent loss of rural employment, while the 1870s and 1880s had seen Ireland losing out in the British market to continental and imperial competitors. However, pressure for improvements in agriculture concentrated on technical instruction, cooperation, quality control, agricultural credit, or the restructuring of uneconomic holdings. These issues were outside the scope of the free trade/protection debate and were capable of being addressed under the Union. No measures were introduced to assist industry, with the exception of technical schools, nor could anything of substance have been done without conflicting with the ideology of the British state.

The treatment afforded to agriculture under the Union was thus infinitely superior to that afforded to industry, a consequence of agriculture's dominance and the complementary needs of the British economy. The fact that the majority of nationalist M.P.'s were dependent on the agricultural electorate consolidated its hold. Agriculture's superiority was given official recognition in the statement of the semiofficial Recess Committee that "agriculture is now, not only the main, but over the greater portion of the country, the sole Irish industry" (Recess Committee 1896, 10).

Any policy for Irish industry would have to take account of agricultural interests, particularly cattle farmers. Many of those disenchanted by the Irish economy under the Union were equally uneasy about the expansion of grazing. As early as the 1840s the agrarian theorist James Fintan Lalor expressed his wish for a country dominated by "a peasantry, not breeders of stock or feeders of fat cattle; not gentlemen who try to be farmers nor farmers who try to be gentlemen but a numerous, plain and home-bred yeomanry" (Lalor 24 Apr., 1844) and this remained a recurrent theme in Irish social thinking, though the postfamine decades saw a sustained expansion of cattle breeding among large and small farmers alike. The radical wing of Irish agrarianism favored expanding the numbers of socially desirable smallholdings rather than of larger cattle farms, though this policy never achieved dominant support in the Irish Parliamentary party. Sinn Fein endeavored to reconcile industrial protection and a more intensive agriculture. D. P. Moran's newspaper, *The Leader,* aspired to the creation of an industrialized and urbanized Ireland coexisting with a modern agricultural sector supporting a stable rural population (Garvin 1987, 114), while Arthur Griffith proposed industrial development plus a contraction of grazing and a substantial increase in tillage, both under protection. He argued that agriculture and industry had identical interests and that both were required to ensure a healthy state (Davis 1974, 128). Such proposals proved attractive to many nationalists because they involved rejecting market forces, which had shifted agriculture to cattle ranching, destroyed Irish industry, and reduced the population. This critical attitude towards economic liberalism also produced a certain ambivalence towards industrialization, despite undoubted concern over Irish industrial decline.

The damage wrought to the Irish economy by nineteenth-century economic developments left some Irish commentators with a decided suspicion of the new age, and Thomas Carlyle appears to have exercised a greater influence than Adam Smith on many Irish minds. Thomas Davis, a poet in the tradition of European romanticism, favored small-scale domestic industry rather than modern factory production (Davis 1989, 186) and his ideas proved surprisingly influential. James Fintan Lalor, a Young Irelander with a more pronounced economic outlook, also denounced the fate of factory workers. "They pass their lives from the cradle to the coffin shut up from the sun and sky and air, working in the furnace and the factory, dwelling in the filthiest lanes of a filthy town, amid everything that is most offensive and disgusting and revolting, an abomination to human feelings and human senses" (Lalor 10 Jan. 1844). Industry conjured up visions of capitalism and city life—matters regarded as alien to Irish society, particularly by Gaelic revivalists and the Yeatsian Celtic Twilight, groups who saw the peasant or small farmer as representing the authentic Irish way of life.

The elevation of the peasant to epitomize the true Irishman reflected the influence of romanticism and the interest in Ireland's past. Those lauding ancient heroism rejected the modern Irish bourgeoisie in favor of the peasants, while Irish language revivalism elevated those who still spoke the language: the illiterate or semiliterate peasantry of the west. The romantic rejection of industry, modernization, materialism and the middle class in favor of the rural, traditional, and spiritual was copper-fastened by an identical rejection process on the part of members of the Anglo-Irish gentry. The intellectual influence of men such as Standish O'Grady or William Butler Yeats ensured that ideas common to their class permeated the Irish cultural vision. The credibility of such ideas was strengthened by their similarity to those held by a substantial body of "educated opinion" in England that stressed "nonindustrial noninnovative and nonmaterial qualities, best encapsulated in rustic imagery" (Wiener 1981, 5–6). The Irish version differed only in its national and, perhaps, religious nuances. Fr. Peter O'Leary, a West Cork Gaelic Leaguer, presented what one writer has termed "a simple-minded, evil-city-versus-virtuous-village polarity, tied up, of course, with an identification of England and English modes with the former and Ireland and Irish-language traditions with the latter" (Garvin 1987, 59). A British Conservative minister of agriculture during the 1920s aimed at "keeping on the land the maximum population the land will support," a policy shared by the Fianna Fail party, while the plea of another Conservative minister, Lord Eustace Percy, for "self-sufficiency as both 'an economic activity not less socially useful than mass production for sale, and as a moral ideal more dignified than the worship of industrial efficiency' " (Wiener 1981, 103, 105) could have been made by Eamon de Valera.

The coincidence of views between such opposing groups reflects the complex interaction of the cultures. Receptiveness of such ideas in Ireland was substantially enhanced because they coincided with the views of the Catholic church (Cahill 1932, 106–52). De Valera's use of the term *frugal comfort,* to describe his aspirations for the Irish population derived from the 1891 encyclical *Rerum Novarum* (Wallace 1966, 272). Irish Catholic clergy feared both socialism and the destructive physical and moral consequences of city life. One priest noted that "the nursery of strong and vigorous men is not in the city but in the country" and argued that "but for the constant influx of rural vigour the inhabitants of a city would die out in the third or fourth generation." Another felt that the solution to urban unemployment lay in breaking up grazing lands and removing people from the city to settle them on smallholdings (Maynooth Union, 1913–14, 1909). Even a wholehearted enthusiast for industry like Arthur Griffith denounced the evils of the factory system and prophesied that electricity would revive domestic industry, leading to small rural industries as opposed to large factories in congested slums (Garvin 1987, 132). This picture encapsulates the socioeconomic vision of many Irish nationalists. Garvin remarks that "the future Ireland of which they dreamed was industrialized, modern, and at the same time culturally authentic in the sense of being a lineal descendant of Gaelic culture. Rural Ireland was to coexist with the cities of the new Ireland as a modernized rural Ireland which retained all its traditional values; Denmark was to come to Knocknagow" (Garvin 1987, 74–75). This desire for small-scale industry coincided with a distaste for modern capitalism, the creator of dark satanic mills and large cities. While Griffith was generally supportive of the employer class, provided they were Irish, as is evidenced in his hostility to the 1913 Lock-Out, others thought in terms of alternative structures such as cooperatives (Garvin 1987, 133; Cahill 1932). The generous public spending of the eighteenth-century Irish parliament was lauded, though many believed that Ireland was overtaxed and were unsympathetic to the social welfare provisions of the pre-1914 Liberal government (Barrington 1987, 39).

The fledgling Irish state therefore inherited a confused baggage of ideals: a desire to protect rural society and its values and to stabilize the rural population; a vision of industrial development minus the evils of capitalism, materialism, and urbanization; a desire to redress previous disadvantages suffered by Irish businesses; an expectation of material progress without state welfare provisions; the restoration of the Irish language and culture; and, though not explicit until the 1920s, the enshrining of Catholic social teaching. Other issues were not clearly addressed, in particular the nature of future economic relations with Britain, how exporting industries would coexist with a protected industrial sector, and how to reconcile cattle farmers and the restoration of tillage. Except for hopes that electricity and motor cars would help to create this economic idyll, no account was taken of the dictates of the market economy. One writer has described the economic visions of the Irish separatists as "wanting to have their cake and eat it" (Garvin 1987, 74–75). The reality was to prove more difficult.

# 2 The Triumph of Continuity, 1922–1927

THE 1920s WERE NOT the most opportune decade for a newly independent nation. Wages and prices fell after wartime inflation; agriculture was depressed; unemployment, external competition, and technological change affected hitherto stable industries; the British economy was in decline, and the neoclassical certainties of free trade and laissez-faire were being questioned. Ireland's chronic problems of emigration, overdependence on agriculture, and a weak industrial sector were accentuated by partition, which removed the most prosperous region and two-thirds of the industrial work force. Add to this the costs of civil war plus the requirement that, unlike British colonies gaining independence in the 1960s who received financial assistance, Ireland was to repay money to Britain, and a difficult scenario emerges.

### The Political Background

Economic policy was constrained by political difficulties. The civil war that erupted in the summer of 1922 caused a split in Sinn Fein, removed many leaders from office, and ensured that security and status dominated the agenda at the expense of socioeconomic questions. The war ended in April 1923 with a victory for pro-treaty[1] forces, however defeated republicans continued to boycott the

1. The Anglo-Irish Treaty, which was signed on 6 Dec. 1921 by representa-

13

institutions of state until 1927 when the Fianna Fail party entered the Dail. While the civil war was fought over nuances in the treaty, it led to a polarization between those desiring change and supporters of the status quo; ultimately the republicans gained their greatest support among the small farmers of the west of Ireland. The Cumann na nGaedheal government was forced to adopt a pro-British attitude on political matters and a conciliatory economic policy. These pressures were reinforced within Dail Eireann where opposition ranks consisted of ex-Unionists, a conservative Farmer's party representing larger farmers, and the Labour party. Pressure within the Dail was more likely to come from the right wing; outside the Dail groups favoring the status quo such as bankers, cattle farmers, and export industries proved more coherent than those wanting change.

The Cumann na nGaedheal government that took office in January 1923 was without any policy save to ensure the survival of the state. It had come into existence by an almost random factor, the remnants of the leadership of the first Dail who had accepted the treaty and survived the civil war. The death of Arthur Griffith in August 1922 removed, in the words of Irish writer George Russell, "the only political leader whose name was associated in the Irish mind with a definite economic policy" and led to uncertainty about the country's economic future (*Irish Statesman* 19 Aug. 1922). His successors were not famed for their economic expertise: the leader, W. T. Cosgrave, had considerable experience in local government; Minister for Finance Ernest Blythe was an Ulster Protestant nationalist interested in Irish language revival; three of the younger members—Home Affairs Minister Kevin O'Higgins, Agriculture Minister Patrick Hogan, and Patrick McGilligan, who became minister for industry and commerce in 1924—had all sat in the same economics class in University College Dublin. The administration was dominated by men who had run the country under Britain and who

---

tives of Dail Eireann and the British government, provided for the establishment of the autonomous Irish Free State. Although Dail Eireann voted to accept the treaty by a narrow margin, civil war broke out between the government and anti-treaty forces in the summer of 1922 and continued until Apr. 1923, ending in government victory.

retained British values and procedures: financial probity, Treasury control, and distaste for economic intervention (Fanning 1978, 57). Civil war gave them increased authority during the formative months of the new state and created long-term financial problems as a consequence of reduced revenue and increased security costs.

In 1923 the state was forced to seek accommodation from Irish banks, who only came to their rescue when ordered to do so by the British Treasury. The Irish Department of Finance subsequently sought to minimize dependence on the banks by minimizing borrowing (Fanning 1978, 88), and this meant an effective veto on new expenditure. The government was forced to befriend a commercial and economic establishment that was dominated by men who had prospered under the Union and who were loath to change.

The continuity of elite in both the private and public sectors reflects the absence of a social revolution and the lack of alternative expertise. While the ranks of former British civil servants contained men such as Joseph Brennan, first secretary of the Department of Finance, who were from Catholic and nationalist traditions, problems with nineteenth-century Catholic university education meant a dearth of such talent. An inquiry from Gordon Campbell, secretary of industry and commerce, to J. G. Smith, professor of commerce at Birmingham University (an Irishman), asking for the names of Irishmen capable of initiating economic development yielded no names (McG Papers P35b/5). With the exception of J. J. McElligott, a former civil servant who left his position as editor of *The Statist* to join the Department of Finance, and T. A. McLaughlin, who masterminded the electricity service, few such men materialized.

### The Irish Economy in the Early Twenties

The economy of the new state remained closely integrated with Britain. Transport and banking links were unchanged, and Britain and Northern Ireland accounted for £50.59 million of total export sales of £51.58 million in 1924. Agriculture employed 670,000 in a total labor force of 1.3 million and agriculture, food, and drink products accounted for 86% of exports in 1924. The economy was, however, depressed following a wartime boom; farmers who had borrowed to buy extra land were saddled with crippling repayments, and net agricultural output by 1924 was 12.6% below the 1914 level (O'Connor and Guiomard 1985, 95). Industry was equally unhealthy, though its status is more difficult to document. The 1912 British Census of Industrial Production recorded 66,693 workers in manufacturing industry in the area that became the Irish Free State (*C. Prod.* 1926; *C. Prod.* 1929, iii, xxi). Britain provided virtually the sole export market for the small number of export firms while British firms competed in the Irish market. Postwar readjustment proved difficult for Irish industry. Firms struggled to reduce wages and other costs, an adjustment exacerbated by the wartime growth in trade union membership from 100,000 to 300,000 by 1920 (Irish Trades Union Congress Report 1920, all-Ireland figures). By 1923 wages in most Irish industries were higher than those in Britain (FIC 1923, app.). The depressed state of British industry and its loss of overseas markets meant increased British competition on the Irish market. Industries such as flour milling and woolens that had operated profitably before 1914 found themselves under acute pressure by the early twenties.

### The Economic Blueprint

The broad sweep of economic policy was determined not by the government but by commissions of experts: the Commission on Agriculture (Agr. 1924), the Fiscal Inquiry Committee (FIC 1923) and Banking Commission (BC 1927). The experts favored the status quo. Ireland would maintain parity and financial links with sterling, produce food for Britain, and retain a free-trade industrial sector.

### Agriculture

The critical role was allocated to agriculture. In a memorandum to the cabinet in January 1924 Agriculture Minister Patrick Hogan emphasized that "national development in Ireland for our generation at least is practically synonymous with agricultural development" (McG Papers P35/b/2), an approach which was accepted by his colleagues. In opting for export-led agriculture, Cumann na nGaedheal accepted the supremacy of market pressures and the need to maintain competitiveness. To this end Hogan urged curbs on local government spending to reduce taxes on farmers, advocated cutting the wages of local authority road workers to prevent pressure on farm laborers' wages, pressed for lower tax levels to increase competitiveness, and urged that farmers be compensated for cost increases consequent on protection (PDDE 23 Jan. 1924). Large farmers were favored at the expense of smallholders and increased spending on unemployment, housing, or industrial development was ruled out.

Hogan's emphasis on financial rectitude and the existing social order held attractions for the Department of Finance and larger farmers. Given that it paralleled the deflationary policies being pursued in Britain it also met the wishes of the Anglo-centric financial establishment. Such a viewpoint led to the decision in 1924 to reduce old-age pensions to permit a reduction in income tax, which was paid by only 60,000 people (Kennedy, Giblin, and McHugh 1988, 36). Hogan's policy entailed an emphasis on cost cutting, education, and quality control. It offered little to those facing emigration or inadequate living standards.

### The Currency Question

This strategy was made more onerous by heavy deflation. The agricultural price index fell from 288 in 1920 to 160 by 1922 and 110 by 1931 (1911–1913 = 100) (Kennedy, Giblin, and McHugh 1988, 36). Deflationary pressures were increased by the decision of the Banking Commission in 1926 that Ireland should retain parity with sterling, a decision that was based on the assumption that Ireland would remain part of the U.K. economic unit (BC 1927), which committed Ireland to an overvalued currency. In a 1924 memorandum to the Cabinet, Joseph Brennan, secretary of the Department of Finance, explained that in the event of Britain returning to the gold standard "on the pre-war basis" the link with sterling would mean deflation and entail surrendering Irish monetary policy into British hands. Brennan questioned whether the country was prepared to accept the consequent depression and unemployment and suggested that agricultural exports and industry would benefit from an Irish currency stabilized at its current depreciated level (S5896, 14 Aug. 1924). While Brennan eventually recommended parity with sterling because of the volume of trade with Northern Ireland and because the First National Loan was denominated in sterling, he suggested that the decision should be reviewed, which was never done.

The 1927 Currency Act established a Saorstat (Free State) pound at parity with sterling, backed by sterling assets. The only criticism of this policy came from the Department of Industry and Commerce. In evidence to the Banking Commission, J. Barrington argued that the deflationary pressures imposed by parity with sterling were more damaging for an agricultural country than for an industrialized economy. Barrington's case was reiterated by Industry and Commerce Secretary Campbell on the occasion of the passing of the 1927 Currency Act where he noted the effect of U.S. deflation on American farmers, adding that "the Saorstat is a country of farmers" (McG Papers P35/a/26).

### The Unemployment Problem

Industry and Commerce were less committed to a policy of continuity than were other economic departments. The Department of Agriculture predated the state and had worked out a role within the British economic model, and Finance had a mission of prudent housekeeping. Industry and Commerce's role was less clear, though its brief included unemployment, the issue which first provoked their dissent. Ireland had inherited the British system of unemployment insurance, which was not designed to cope with long-term unemployment. By the end of 1922 the system was in disarray as insured workers exhausted their benefits and others had not accumulated sufficient credits to earn benefits. Gordon Campbell, secretary of industry and commerce, proposed establishing a reconstruction commission to determine the true level of unemployment and to recommend means of tackling it with a substantial budget of £2 million. The Cabinet approved his report, but the question of allocating extra funds was referred to the Department of Finance and subsequently withdrawn (S1906). An interim report by the Commission on Reconstruction in 1923 recommending a five-year program of road works to relieve unemployment was dismissed by the Cabinet as impracticable (Gaughan 1980, 243). Industry and Commerce's concern with unemployment continued, however. The department estimated that by February 1924 there would be 80,000 workers with "no work, no benefit and little or no prospect of any private employment," a figure that excluded many republican prisoners about to be released (McG Papers P35/b/1). A similar crisis in London led British Prime Minister Stanley Baldwin to call a general election in an abortive effort to gain a mandate for protection, an event whose outcome was anxiously watched in Dublin (S3439). Industry and Commerce proposed introducing protection to relieve unemployment plus a Trade Facilities Act to provide government guarantees for long-term loans to industry, a measure operating in Britain since 1920 (S4278 10 Dec. 1923).

### The Introduction of Tariff Protection

Fiscal independence would have held few practical consequences before 1914 as Britain was a free trade country; however, during World War I the British government introduced selective protective duties. In 1922, Britain, the Irish Free State, and Northern Ireland had operated as a fiscal unit with taxation divided proportionately, and protection first emerged as a political issue with the threatened onset of Irish fiscal independence in April 1923. Fiscal separation from the United Kingdom meant that Irish exports to Britain of protected commodities became subject to British import duties, and all imports into Ireland became dutiable at the same rates as goods imported into Britain. These duties made the option of continuity that existed for both agriculture and banking considerably less feasible for trade and industry.

With civil war still in progress, the Irish state was forced to decide on a protective policy to which it had given no prior thought. The Department of Finance apparently accepted the British schedule of duties but objected to granting preferential rates to the empire.

Both Industry and Commerce and the North East Boundary Bureau[2] urged using tariffs as a tool for industrial development. Lionel Smith-Gordon of the North East Boundary Bureau argued for adopting a different schedule of duties from Britain's, believing that "﹄nless we take an independent line from the beginning we shall rapidly become an 'economic suburb of England' " (S2402). Several of the industrialists directly affected such as distiller Andrew Jameson, George Jacobs of the biscuit firm, brewer George McArdle, and tobacco producer J. E. Carroll were members of a Chamber of Commerce delegation that sought to postpone the customs barrier (*IT* 2 Mar. 1923). Their objections were read by Kevin O'Sheil of the North East Boundary Bureau as politically motivated, reflecting the views of "the old reactionary and anti-national elements" (Blythe Papers P7/c/156). However, Sheil's estimate ignored Irish industry's traditional free access to the British market and industrialists' awareness that minimal fiscal changes would result in major disruption.

Such negative consequences were most evident in the case of the Ford plant in Cork, which was part of the company's U.K. operation, built on the assumption that parts and equipment could move freely between the two countries (Jacobson 1977, 23). By 1923 Ford employed 1,600 workers and paid weekly wages of £10,000. Irish fiscal independence meant that cars or parts imported from Britain faced a duty of 22.2%, and a similar duty was payable on exports from Ireland to Britain. For Ford, the solution was simple. The manager in Cork pointed out the consequences of closing the plant, adding that "we feel quite sure that when the government realise the magnitude of the issues involved they will take the necessary steps to negotiate some form of trade treaty with England that will provide for the termination of the prohibitive duty on our manufacturing goods entering England" (S4427). But, such a move would involve abandoning all pretense at fiscal independence, a point recognized by most speakers in a Senate debate on the Ford problem (PDSE 21 Mar.

2. A government body established to make propaganda for the largest possible transfer of territory from Northern Ireland to the Irish Free State by the Boundary Commission. Under the terms of the 1921 Anglo-Irish Treaty the Boundary Commission was to determine the boundaries between both parts of Ireland. In 1925 the British and Irish governments agreed to suppress its findings and to accept existing borders (O'Halloran 1987, xiii; Lee 1989, 140–51).

1923) and expressed more forcibly by government advisor Joseph Johnston who noted that "any argument based on the effect of the Customs barrier on Messrs. Ford's activity in Cork would be arguments in favour not of a temporary postponement of the barriers but of abandoning it and our fiscal freedom forever" (S2405).

Faced with conflicting advice the government opted to retain all British duties unchanged. This decision resulted in a ragbag of duties that bore no relation to Irish needs, hardly the hallmark of a government exercising economic independence. The decision may have been influenced by the British announcement that imperial preference would apply to imports from Ireland; however, the absence of taxation changes in the Irish budget some weeks later was viewed by the *Economist* as "marking time" (28 Apr. 1923), and it was presumably unease about the decision that prompted the establishment in June of the the Fiscal Inquiry Committee to report on the effect of the existing fiscal system on industry and agriculture and on any changes intended to foster industrial and agricultural development.

### The Fiscal Inquiry Committee

The Fiscal Inquiry Committee was subsequently described by one of its members, economic historian George O'Brien, whose brief was limited to agricultural issues (S3107) as "heavily in favour of free trade" (Meenan 1980, 128). It was dominated by C. F. Bastable, professor of economics at Trinity College Dublin and "a survivor of the great days of Victorian liberalism when free trade was regarded by British economists as a religion rather than a policy" (Meenan, 1980, 128). Whereas the reports of the Commission on Agriculture and the Banking Commission reflected the thrust of the evidence, the Fiscal Inquiry Committee's recommendation of free trade was at variance with the overwhelming majority of witnesses who demanded protection. The only exceptions were the maltsters, jute manufacturers, Jacobs (the biscuit firm), printers, and Cork Teachta Dalas. A. O'Shaughnessy and Prof. A. O'Rahilly who argued the interests of Ford.

One supporter of protection subsequently noted that "close on forty Irish manufacturing industries gave evidence before the Fiscal

Inquiry Committee in support of protective tariffs, and each one of these, with one trifling exception, were prejudiced or damnified by the Report, not upon the merits of each case, but upon general principles" (PDDE 15 Feb. 1924). The absence of the banks, chambers of commerce, Ford, and Guinness was viewed by the committee as signifying approval of the status quo, and their unvoiced opinions received considerably greater weight than did the opinions of those who attended. On this basis it was concluded that "the volume of industry which is anxious to obtain a protective tariff is small compared with that which desires no change in the existing system." Tariffs were condemned as raising prices and costs with adverse impact on exports and employment (FIC pars. 119–20). There was no minority report, so the message of free trade and the priority afforded to agriculture and export industries was not challenged. In retrospect, George O' Brien conceded that "in regard to manufacturers, some concession might have perhaps been prudently made to sentiment. . . . There was a widespread desire, not only among the businessmen who would have duly profited, but among the public generally for some attempt to revive Irish industry. If the Committee had indicated the directions in which such an attempt could be most safely and least expensively made, its reports would probably have received more respect and would have led to positive action" (Meenan 1980, 129).

The apparently partisan report led to increased pressure for protection. Many of the lobbyists had been pioneers of local industrial development associations and members of Sinn Fein, and this increased their bitterness. One contributor to the government newspaper, *The Gael*, asked "is advocating Arthur Griffith's policy treason to the Free State?" (Blythe Papers, P7/c/56). Individual industries presented their case in isolation and the Fiscal Inquiry Committee criticized the lack of cohesion in the protectionist camp (FIC par. 66).

The Dublin Industrial Development Association (DIDA) did not give evidence but elected to help individual groups prepare their case, a decision that reflected a split within its ranks. It refused to join the protectionist Federation of Irish Industries on the grounds that neither was it a "free trade body" nor was it "committed to indiscriminate protection" (National Agricultural and Industrial Development Association 1905–1935, 29). The arbitrary dismissal of protection by the Fiscal Inquiry Committee tilted the balance of opinion in the DIDA. Its annual report for 1923 condemned "the non-judicial and extraordinary manner in which the great weight of evidence in favour of some form of protection was brushed aside by the Fiscal Inquiry Committee while all who abstained from tendering evidence were, for no very cogent reason, assumed to agree with the present system of free imports" (DIDA minutes 10 Aug. 1923, report Dec. 1923). DIDA endorsed protection in February 1924 and urged others to follow suit. However the Irish Industrial Development Association (IIDA), the body responsible for the Irish trademark, refused, arguing that it would alienate their Northern Ireland trademark users, a decision that deprived the protectionist camp of access to the IIDA's substantial income (DIDA minutes Feb. 1924, report 1924–1925).

The government distanced itself from the criticism directed at the report because W. T. Cosgrave had stated that "the committee is not expected to advocate policy. That will be a matter for the people and the government when they have the facts before them" (PDDE 15 June 1923). The unofficial response was a search for a middle ground. This was signaled by the minister for industry and commerce, Joseph McGrath, in the Dail when he promised limited protection that would not injure agriculture with the emphasis on products with a large domestic market. However, he added that "the onus of proof" lay with "the advocates of Protection," ruling out any prospect of "a fiscal revolution" and denying that Ireland's destiny lay in becoming "a concentrated industrial region" (PDDE 21 Jan. 1924).

### Tariff Policy 1924-1926

McGrath's policy was apparently endorsed by the cabinet, though not by J. J. McElligott, assistant secretary of finance. His memorandum to Finance Minister Blythe in response to McGrath's speech argued that protection once granted could never be reversed and would inevitably entail further protection, "a medicine that needs to be taken in large doses" (Fanning 1978, 203–4). McElligott suggested that the government concentrate on reducing wages.

On 29 February Industry and Commerce submitted a paper on tariffs for cabinet consideration. In a covering letter Campbell prophesied "a consistent fall in the volume of manufacturing industry," with consequent impact on banks and shopkeepers and potential "danger to the well-being of the State if a progressive remedy be not speedily applied." The accompanying report provided a bullish account of the potential benefits of protection. It rejected the argument that industries that were compelled to import raw materials were not "natural" industries worthy of assistance—citing Belfast shipbuilders Harland and Wolff, Guinness, and Lancashire cotton as arguments to the contrary. The case against tariffs on cost-of-living grounds was dismissed by providing that tariffs be withdrawn in the event of abuse, while increased customs revenue could be used to reduce other taxes. The report envisaged tariffs leading to the establishment of factories by "some of the best organized external manufacturing concerns" with benefits to employment, taxes, and national standards of manufacture and argued that protection would ultimately generate new exports and better shipping. Detailed information was appended on fifteen industries that could be protected without serious impact on the cost of living.[3] The report concluded with the cry, to be repeated by Campbell on many future occasions, that "a bold, well-conceived policy, which would result in extending industrial activity in this country, is essential if the state is to prosper. Otherwise, we must remain dependent on agriculture to keep the State afloat. This latter alternative means putting all our eggs in one basket, the bottom of which is by no means secure" (F22/11/24). The timing of this memorandum is significant. By this time Joseph McGrath, the minister for industry and commerce, was in fundamental disagreement with the majority of the cabinet over army demobilization and was to resign on 7 March (Fanning 1983, 48). In consequence the report never reached the cabinet.

McGrath's replacement by Patrick McGilligan appears to have led to a cooling of protectionist ardor. On 19 March Campbell wrote to both McElligott and to the secretary of the executive council

---

3. F. 22/11/24. Tariff proposals for the Saorstat. Soap, soap powders and candles, glass bottles, boots and shoes, apparel, hosiery and woolen textiles, furniture, railway rolling stock, cars and wagons, commercial motor bodies, bicycles, cement, horn beads and combs, margarine, and sugar confectionery.

disengaging from the explicitly protectionist stance but requesting that the matter be debated by the cabinet, taking account of unemployment, the effect on prices, and "all counterbalancing advantages to be secured from industrial development." No such debate occurred though the matter was referred to government officials. In a letter to Blythe dated 9 April 1924, Patrick Hogan, minister for agriculture, noted recent discussions with Gordon Campbell concerning a proposal to impose tariffs on two or three items. Campbell had complained that he had made several abortive efforts to initiate a discussion on tariff policy, and he felt "without having some definite policy, it is quite impossible to pick out three or four items and say we will protect them." As an alternative he proposed establishing a Tariff Commission. Unlike the Fiscal Inquiry Committee "this Commission would start with the presumption that tariffs were to be imposed, and important tariffs, examine the question, show the results in detail, and the Government could then make up its mind." Hogan endorsed Campbell's proposal, but it received short shrift from McElligott, who claimed that it was "rather absurd that after one Government Committee turned down tariffs, another Committee should be set up to establish them" (F22/11/24). Campbell's request for a policy debate was evaded.

The 1924 budget imposed tariffs on boots and shoes, confectionery, soap and candles, bottles, and commercial motor bodies; in Hogan's opinion "unimportant things" as opposed to "things that really matter such as textiles, clothing," and tariff levels were below those suggested by Industry and Commerce. The impact of tariffs on the cost of living remained a major concern, and to compensate for the anticipated increase the duty on tea was reduced (PDDE 25 Apr. 1924).

The 1925 budget brought tariffs on clothing, blankets, furniture, and bedsteads. Blythe reiterated government opposition to a general tariff, justifying the new impositions on the grounds that the tariffs of the previous year had offered too limited a basis for determining fiscal policy. He also announced that no further tariffs would be imposed before the country could express its opinion in a general election. The threat to agriculture from higher prices was advanced as an argument against further protection (PDDE 22 Apr. 1925).

External pressure kept the tariff debate alive. In February 1925 the Dublin Industrial Development Association organized a Joint Industrial Council of manufacturers and trade unionists, which passed a resolution demanding that imports in a wide range of industries be restricted to 50% of their current level, with a 25% tariff on the balance (DIDA minutes, 23 Feb., 11 Mar. 1925). Labour party leader Tom Johnson suggested the establishment of a committee or commission to inquire into the effect of tariffs, prompting a commitment from Blythe to establish a "formal tribunal" "in the course of a year or so" (PDDE 23 Apr., 24 Apr. 1925). By June officials were contemplating draft proposals for a Watchdog Committee on Tariffs and scrutinizing Dail statements in an effort to interpret ministerial intentions. Initial proposals provided for a large committee representing agriculture, labor, banking, commerce, and industry to "consider" the effects of tariffs. The proposal aroused instant hostility among Finance officials who criticized its vagueness and objected to a committee reporting to the executive council rather than to a minister (F22/44/25). The idea lapsed until mid-1926 when it was reconsidered in response to renewed pressure from both agriculture and industry.

Industrial demands were channeled through the Department of Industry and Commerce, which held regular meetings with committees representing more than thirty industries (ITJ Nov. 1925). Nineteen requested tariffs in 1926. The applications had a common theme: owing to international depression, dumping, and increased British competition, the collapse of industries that had prospered and often exported before 1914. Tanning had declined from twenty factories before 1914 to six that mostly worked part-time. Both margarine and agricultural machinery had lost substantial export markets. Allegations of prejudice against Irish products were common: the Woollen Manufacturers Association claimed that "all the sentiment in the country which favoured the Irish article is dead and the Irish Manufacturer has suffered in consequence." Industry and Commerce distanced itself from such representations. A letter to Finance pointed out that the applications originated from the industries, and their role was limited to scrutinizing figures and summoning meetings of advisory committees.

Applications were considered by an interdepartmental committee representing Finance, revenue commissioners, Agriculture and Industry and Commerce. Procedural objections from the revenue commissioners were common, and the Department of Agriculture lodged formal objections in all cases save mineral oils, brushes, and corsets—a possible insight into farmers' consumption habits. For items such as rosary beads, briar pipes, and down quilts Agriculture noted the possibility of "some increase in the cost of living without any compensating benefit to the farmer"; in cases such as agricultural machinery their objections were more detailed. They condemned a proposed tariff on woolens because of farmers' needs for good, strong, quality clothing "to withstand the hard wear on the farm" and their fear of "a tendency on the part of the agricultural community to buy unsuitable materials or low priced ready-made suits" (F39/6/26). Finance adopted an almost neutral attitude but sought guidance from the government. Joseph Brennan told his minister that "it would be useful at this stage if an indication could be given as to how far the Government think it worthwhile pursuing further investigations of any of these proposals." He was particularly concerned about the political implications where the industry consisted of a single firm, such as agricultural machinery. This plea for political direction was again left unanswered.

The campaign for protection was not limited to discreet applications from industrial groups. While the Department of Agriculture presented a solid case against protection, the balance of opinion within the farming community was shifting. Agricultural depression and disastrous weather (O'Connor and Guiomard 1985, 95–97) led some farmers to seek protection in the hope of averting a steady fall in grain acreage. In August 1925 a conference held by Kildare County Committee of Agriculture recommended a tariff on wheat, oats, and barley and experimental trials to extend wheat acreage. A deputation sought meetings with the ministers for finance and agriculture: both refused, and the chairman of Kildare County Committee of Agriculture, J. J. Bergin, established a Grain Growers Association to campaign for tariffs on grain products. The adjoining county of Laoighis passed a resolution demanding a tariff on barley (F22/65/25), while the Wexford branch of Cumann na nGaedheal sought a tariff on cement (F22/63/25). The protariff campaign of the Cork Industrial Development Association was supported by Senator James Dowdall and by J. J. Walsh, minister for posts and telegraphs (*IT* 23 Mar. 1926). While Hogan refused repeated requests to meet with the Grain Growers Association, Walsh remained in close contact with it (F22/57/25). By 1926 he was chairman of the party and consequently a figure of some influence. Nor was he an isolated figure. It appears from their contributions in the Dail that several other T.D.'s, notably Dublin deputies Denis McCullough and Prof. Michael Tierney, were also sympathetic towards protection.

Public opinion was divided. The announcement by the minister for finance in January 1926 that he was considering extending protection to agriculture resulted in a resolution from the annual meeting of the Irish Farmers' Union reminding the government that it had no mandate for such action (*IT* 26 Jan., 18 Mar. 1926). The budget submission from the Association of Chambers of Commerce sought further reductions in income tax, an end to corporation profits tax, and a "Geddes-style" committee to curb government spending (F39/2/26). In the face of competing demands Blythe's 1926 budget imposed only one tariff on oats, which may have been a symbolic gesture to agriculture. He explained that under present "abnormal" conditions some manufacturers were unlikely to survive for a further two years, by which time the government might have a mandate for protection, and announced the establishment of a Tariff Commission to investigate proposals for further protection (PDDE 21 Apr. 1926).

*The Tariff Commission*

The announcement brought a division in government ranks, with Walsh speaking in favor of protection both in the Dail and elsewhere (*IT* 26 May 1926), though he ultimately voted for the measure, while Minister for Home Affairs Kevin O'Higgins countered with a speech endorsing the status quo. Prof. William Magennis (PDDE 30 July 1926) alleged in a speech that the matter had been the subject of heated discussion at the party conference in May 1926 (of which Walsh was chairman), and although newspaper coverage of this event is scant, divisions of opinion over tariffs are not in doubt (*IT* 12 May 1926). O'Higgins was undoubtedly hostile to protection, as was Hogan, who was concerned with export competitiveness of agriculture. The attitude of McGilligan is less obvious. In a debate on Industry and Commerce estimates in 1925 he stressed that "it is not the function of the Dail directly and immediately to provide employment. Certain pressure could be put on people, and certain tendencies could be developed, and then certain adjustments in the fiscal system could be made so as to ensure as far as we can ensure without interfering directly with trade or enterprises that there would be more employment; but beyond that we cannot go; we cannot enter into the field of state interference or state control of industry" (PDDE 31 Oct. 1925). It may seem paradoxical that these views were expressed by the man who masterminded the major economic intervention of the Cumann na nGaedheal government— the Shannon electrification scheme and the state-owned Electricity Supply Board. McGilligan had a fear of private monopoly, which led him to favor the lesser evil of a state electrical monopoly. However, the same fear of monopoly or lack of competitive discipline led him to mistrust protection. By 1926 the proposed Tariff Commission held the attraction of depoliticizing the issue.

The initial draft of the Tariff Commission bill emanated from Industry and Commerce on 17 April, four days before Blythe's Dail announcement. The minister for finance was given the sole power of referring applications to the commission and the right to nominate both secretary and chairman. The commission was to report to him, and he would impose tariffs in the light of its recommendations, subject to Dail resolution. We can only guess at the motives behind Industry and Commerce's self-denial with respect to tariff policy. McGilligan may have regarded the successful completion of the Shannon scheme, which had been undertaken in the teeth of Finance's hostility (Fanning 1978, 178–86; Manning and McDowell 1984, chaps. 3, 4), as a higher priority. Campbell excluded himself from serving on the Tariff Commission on the grounds that the Shannon scheme was taking the greater part of his time as he was "the only person available who has sufficient knowledge of the scheme and can effectively be made responsible for the necessarily centralised supervision" (McG Papers P35/39). The outcome was a downgrading of Industry and Commerce that was to last until 1932.

The proposal to cede control to Finance was greeted with less than enthusiasm by the recipient. Joseph Brennan viewed the establishment of commissions substituting for "efficient Departmental advice" as "a distinctly retrograde step." He was aware of the political dimensions of the controversy but saw the commission as subjecting civil servants' policy making to public gaze. "Advice to Ministers on matters of administrative policy is shielded from publicity. Apart from the advantage this ensures that in matters which lend themselves to party controversy Ministers are not embarrassed if the official advice tended to them conflicts with party interests for the time being. It is probably inevitable that the larger tariff questions should form party issues in this country for some time to come and it seems inevitable that civil servants should be put in a position where they could be publicly recognised as forming or opposing the intentions of a particular party."

Blythe ignored Brennan's objections and requested that he suggest "any clauses for a Bill setting up a Tariff Commission which would give the maximum of direction to a Commission consistent with what I said in the Budget statement." Brennan's reply exposed the proposed commission and lack of government policy to merciless scrutiny. He noted that before clauses could be drafted it was "necessary to reach a clear understanding of the substance of the policy." He toyed with the option of directing the commission to follow precedents established in existing tariffs but decided that "such a form of word would scarcely convey any real guidance owing to the difficulty, not to say impossibility of tracing a clear principle in those enactments." He concluded that Blythe's budget speech appeared to imply that tariffs should only be granted to preserve existing industries, which if extended beyond antidumping measures "would seem to open the door for the most questionable of all cases of protection, i.e. when an industry is not nascent but decaying" (F22/44/25).

The Tariff Commission came into existence without political guidance under legislation closely modeled on the British Safeguarding of Industry Act, drafted to prevent applications by bodies such as the DIDA or the Council of Saorstat Manufacturers. Only persons substantially representative of those engaged in or proposing to engage in an industry could apply. Campbell informed Brennan that McGilligan considered this restriction important. Hogan proposed that the ministers for agriculture and for industry and commerce could initiate applications; he also felt that the measure should allow for the prospect of assisting industries by other means such as export bounties. Such extensions were rejected, and the measure was virtually identical to the first draft save for the deletion of the proposal that tariffs could be introduced by administrative order—a proposal denounced by Joseph Brennan as "without parallel so far as I know in the practice of at least any of the better governed states of the world"; each tariff was to be the subject of specific legislation. The ambiguity of the government's approach was evident in Blythe's speech on the second reading of the bill, which he began by stating that with the bill's passage "we shall have said good-bye to doctrinaire free trade," adding that "for the future applications or proposals for the imposition of tariffs would be examined more minutely and in a more formal and deliberate way than has been the case in the past." Most deputies saw the measure as a delaying tactic pending a general election (PDDE 30 June 1926).

### *The Triumph of Exporting Agriculture*

Following the Tariff Commission's establishment the major economic intiatives appeared to be directed towards assisting agricultural interests, as articulated by Patrick Hogan. Hogan's belief in the overriding interests of agriculture and his antipathy towards state aid for industry appear to have hardened during his years in office. In 1925 he and McGilligan contemplated a joint program for state-assisted credit for both agriculture and industry. A partly state-financed Agricultural Credit Corporation was established, but assistance to industry was limited to the 1923 trade loans guarantee scheme (Daly 1984a). By 1927 he had evolved a justification of state aid for agriculture on the grounds of agriculture's central position in the economy, while demanding that farmers be compensated for any assistance given to industry. This was explicitly stated in a memorandum to the executive council in January 1927 when Hogan obtained substantial funds to restructure the dairy industry, expenditure justified in terms of national interest. The memorandum stated that tariffs imposed a burden on agriculture for which farmers should be compensated, a view that appears to have gone unchallenged within the cabinet, but one that aroused strong objections from Industry and Commerce Secretary Gordon Campbell.

In a memorandum to McGilligan, also dated January 1927, Campbell criticized Hogan's espousal of "mixed farming" as "a form which supports a low proportion of persons, which produces a relatively small volume of wealth, and which is very sensitive to conditions in other countries on which it is necessarily dependent. It may be an inevitable con-comitant of land division at its present stage. But it will not increase the population nor produce the maximum wealth possible nor be stable unless conditions in Britain are stable" (McG Papers P36/b/9). Campbell proposed assisting agriculture by protection, subsidies, or guaranteed prices to encourage domestic processing of agricultural products. While this strategy was seen as carrying inherent risks, he felt that it would increase rural population and produce increased wealth and greater internal stability. Campbell was endeavoring to reconcile the interests of agriculture and industry by weaning agriculture from doctrinaire free trade. His reasoning reflected the interests of aspirant Irish industry and his innate scepticism about the effectiveness of a development strategy that relied on agriculture. On another occasion he argued that undue dependence on agriculture tied the Irish economy to a life of instability; agricultural countries tended, he argued, to be impoverished and gave little scope for talented individuals such as university graduates. These memoranda were followed by Campbell's attack, already noted, on the 1927 decision to adopt parity with sterling.

Although it can be argued that Campbell was stepping beyond the normal functions of a civil servant and attempting to formulate policy, the point is moot. His arguments were too late. The institution of a Tariff Commission under Finance control had removed the most critical policy area from Industry and Commerce. Campbell's proposals would have required the abolition of the Tariff Commission within months of its constitution. There is no evidence that McGilligan accepted Campbell's arguments, or that they ever reached the cabinet. By 1927 Cumann na nGaedheal's economic policy was committed towards continuing the postfamine pattern of close trading connections with Britain with consequent emphasis on agriculture and food-based export industries—a beer, biscuits, cars, and cattle coalition—and on a continuing sterling link. Tariff protection had been depoliticized and was no longer on the agenda.

This state of affairs is evident from the Cumann na nGaedheal platform in the 1927 general election. Despite earlier commitments to put the issue to the electorate, the party's campaign advertisements in June 1927 avoided commitments on protection and emphasized their record in reducing taxation, increasing agricultural rates relief, improving the quality of agricultural produce, and investing in roads and housing. They also mentioned the construction of the largest sugar factory in Europe, the potential of the Shannon scheme to revolutionize Irish industry, and the help given "as far as lay in its power (to) many struggling industries in their fight against foreign competition. Over thirty new factories had been established giving employment to 10,000 workers." Future commitments to industry were limited to promises to promote "industrial and commercial development through confidence of investors" (*IT* 1 June, 4 June 1927). In the June 1927 election Cumann na nGaedheal returned 47 members, one more than the new Fianna Fail party, compared with 63 in 1923.

The electoral rebuff brought no change in industrial policy. Contentment with the status quo and a dearth of new ideas are the hallmarks of McGilligan's speech on the estimates for Industry and Commerce shortly after the convening of the new Dail. He reported that his officials had been investigating the possibility of establishing new industries, had initiated contacts between foreign firms and Irish businessmen, and had toured the country to promote local initiative. There is no evidence that these measures had borne fruit, and his claim that "in every possible way that a Government department can intervene there has been intervention with a view to getting local capital and enterprise joined to start new industries" (PDDE 30 June 1927) was not endorsed by Campbell.

In a memorandum to McGilligan written shortly before the above speech and perhaps designed to influence its tone, Campbell argued that given Irish disabilities such as a small home market, lack of industrial training, and an absence of indigenous resources, industrial development or even a "better balance between agriculture and industry" was impossible without substantial government involvement.

> Stimulation there must be and it will inevitably take forms open to objection if measured solely by the criteria current in prosperous countries with large resources and established manufactures. Unless therefore it is definitely decided as a cardinal point of policy that industrial development must be earnestly

attempted it is no use undertaking the difficult and often tedious and disappointing inquiries and negotiations required to devise effective means of stimulation. If comparative heterodoxy (judged by British standards) is to bar every proposal made with this object from serious consideration it would be a waste of time thinking out proposals. Unless assured that the Government was prepared to pay a price for early industrial development there is no incentive to work out a basis for it in the certain knowledge that every such basis must, in the existing circumstances of the country, involve payment of a price in the form of a tariff, subsidy, bounty, special credit or other fiscal adjustment. The contiguity of Ireland to Great Britain should not obscure the fact that in all the smaller countries it has been, since the war, a recognised necessity for Governments to take a greatly increased share of responsibility in measures for the direct promotion of industry.

Campbell suggested that the department hire industrial investigators who would negotiate with foreign industrialists with a view to establishing Irish plants. New export markets should be investigated, state funding should be provided for a "buy Irish" campaign, while conferences should be held with Irish industrialists. He proposed inquiries into the difficulties of locating factories outside the major towns, the initiating of tariff proposals by Industry and Commerce, and the establishment of a standing committee of the executive council responsible for industrial development "not merely to consider proposals put before it but to call itself for proposals and see that it gets them" (McG Papers P35/b/10).

Export promotion was already being funded on a modest scale. That Campbell's other proposals were not considered is not surprising as they were never brought before the Cabinet. McGilligan's speech implicitly rejected Campbell's views, with his optimistic account of the department's activities and the statement that "the whole matter of Government initiative of industrial development in this country is not one I should like to pronounce upon at this time." The only proposal endorsed by McGilligan was a "buy Irish" campaign to be organized by an outside body such as the DIDA (PDDE 30 June 1927).

## Conclusion

This speech marks the final occasion when McGilligan was wholly preoccupied with Industry and Commerce. In July 1927 Kevin O'Higgins was assassinated; emergency legislation forced Fianna Fail to take its seats or lose them to also-rans; and the government called a general election in which Fianna Fail and Cumann na nGaedheal increased their representation at the expense of smaller parties, leaving Cumann na nGaedheal with a small majority. The election brought the departure of J. J. Walsh, whose letter of resignation announced that he would not be contesting the forthcoming election because of the government's stance on protection. Walsh accused the Tariff Commission of being determined "to produce arguments in favour of Free Trade" and alleged that Cumann na nGaedheal "has gone bodily over to the most reactionary elements of the state who will henceforth control its policies. Followers of Arthur Griffith's economic teaching will now be forced to subordinate their life-long conviction to the dictates of people whose only concern appears to be the welfare of England." Walsh charged that the election should be concerned with "a disappearing population, disappearing trade and rapidly sinking bank reserves," matters necessitating "vigorous and sweeping economic change" as opposed to "oaths, loans and what Mr. So and So did or said in such and such a year" (S5470). Walsh was an isolated figure. His departure removed one of the most entrepreneurial spirits from the party, though he had been preceded, albeit for noneconomic reasons, by Joe Mc Grath, minister for industry and commerce, who was to establish one of the largest business empires of the new state. It would appear that Cumann na nGaedheal was ill at ease with those who sought to build private fortunes in the new state. The government rejected proposals from some of its supporters for the establishment of a private broadcasting service in favor of the state-controlled Radio Eireann and opposed efforts by commercial interests to build a hydroelectric station on the river Liffey in favor of the state's Shannon scheme (Manning and McDowell 1984, 29–30).

Richard Mulcahy, who had left the cabinet with McGrath in 1924, though he returned in 1927, claimed in later years that the loss of McGrath, Walsh, O'Higgins, and himself had "left the directing force, in the parliamentary party and in the government completely denuded of those people and names who stood for the Griffith approach and policy, in relation to industrial development (Fanning 1983, 102). However, Griffith's policies had never been dominant in Cumann na nGaedheal nor had they been supported by O'Higgins, and they had lost out partly because of the power of established interests but also because no occupant of a key economic ministry, save possibly Joseph McGrath, articulated them. Continuity triumphed because of this vacuum. Joseph Brennan's repeated pleas for some direction on tariff policy remained unheeded. Protectionist forces were weak and disorganized, leaving free trade interests with no serious competition.

# 3 Protection, Intervention, and Economic Crisis, 1927–1932

THE YEARS 1927–1932 WERE MARKED by a growing polarization on economic issues within Dail Eireann, played out against a backdrop of international depression from 1929. Emigration reached its highest level in forty years, and allegations of distress and unemployment were rife, though difficult to prove because of inadequate statistics. On the whole Cumann na nGaedheal clung to economic orthodoxy and the party's economic and social policies were characterized by procrastination. The only new social program undertaken was the reform of the Poor Law, though political pressure forced an improved housing program in 1931. By 1927 there had been three consecutive years of budgetary surplus; per capita national debt amounted to $39.54 and debt servicing took 5.18% of revenue (S5563). Both taxes and expenditure fell marginally from 1926 to 1931 though public debt rose from £14.1 million in 1926 to £29.3 million in 1931. (Meenan 1970, 254). The government remained committed to a free-trading agriculture and took measures to assist it, but agricultural output at its 1929/30 peak remained 4% below the prewar level, and net output was 5% below the 1924/25 level (Kennedy, Giblin, and McHugh 1988, 37).

Intervention in agriculture brought undesired results. Hopes of establishing a cooperative agricultural credit agency and of turning the restructured creameries over to cooperative ownership proved fruitless and the government was left, somewhat unwillingly, with two state enterprises, while a ten-year subsidy and tax concessions to

37

a Belgian firm to process beet sugar resulted in company profits of £200,000 for 1927–29 on £400,000 share capital and dividends of 10–15%—giving rise to considerable criticism as the annual burden on the consumer was approximately £900,000 (S4128). While demands for agricultural protection brought a relaxation of the official position on tariffs and eased the path for industry, the lesson that intervention could result in long-term government involvement or excessive profits increased the reluctance to intervene in industry.

*The Impact of Fianna Fail*

From 1927 the government faced powerful opposition from the Fianna Fail party. In its founding constitution Fianna Fail showed its continuity with traditional Sinn Fein thinking, reiterating the belief that Ireland could flourish under independence and calling for industrial development behind protective tariffs, programs of reforestation, transport, land distribution, and a state development bank. While initial commitments were vague (Rumpf and Hepburn, 1977, 100–102) the program was gradually refined. The party argued that Ireland could support a substantially higher population by abandoning international living standards and by defying conventional economic maxims (PDDE 13 July 1928). It favored self-sufficiency, exploitation of native resources, and increased government intervention to be funded through administrative economies and through an end to the payment of land annuities to the British Exchequer.

This program was honed in a series of confrontations that emphasized the gulf between government and opposition. The divisions encompassed attitudes towards the 1921 treaty, relations with Britain, and the broad thrust of Irish independence. The economic divisions were of a piece with those on the national question: between continuity and change; between retaining close links with Britain and asserting independence; between introspective isolation—even breaking with economic conventions—and a more international outlook. The contrasting positions may have served to entrench each party in its particular ideological camp.

*Protection: The Tariff Commission*

Initially the Tariff Commission achieved its unstated purpose of slowing protectionist momentum, though several decisions were ill advised and may have been politically determined. Despite lengthy deliberations its tariffs proved less effective in stimulating domestic output than the less-considered efforts of earlier years. Disproportionate attention was devoted to trivial industries, from the first report on rosary beads to the final report on prayer books, with fish barrels and down quilts, an industry employing sixty workers, among those also considered.

The first two reports, granting protection to rosary beads and margarine, were issued promptly, causing the *Economist* to speculate that they had been deliberately engineered to upstage Fianna Fail (26 Nov. 1927); thereafter procrastination ruled. By the autumn of 1930 when the commission was reconstituted only eight reports had been completed. In addition to rosary beads and margarine, tariffs were granted to down quilts and to manufacturers of certain grades of woolen cloth but were refused for fish barrels, motor bodies, flour, and paper products (TC 1927–1930, R 36/1–8). Whether the delays were deliberate or an inevitable consequence of the commission's composition (three senior civil servants with other demanding duties) is unclear. An application for a tariff on motor vehicles in January 1927 was not completed until November 1930 when it was rejected, though the government granted protection to cars and motor parts in 1928; a report on paper and packaging took three years; one on leather, four. Such delays seem at variance with the statement accompanying the commission's establishment in 1926, which emphasized that some industries could not wait until tariff policy was determined by a general election. Yet by 1930 Blythe stated that he did not regard eighteen months as an excessive delay (PDDE 19 Feb. 1930), though one applicant for a tariff on leather ceased trading before the report was complete and the Clondalkin paper mill closed while protection for paper was being considered.

Our knowledge of the Tariff Commission is severely handicapped by the nonavailability of its working files, and many relevant Finance files are missing or were destroyed during the emergency of

1939–1945 when paper was recycled. Lists of missing files indicate that the number of applications for protection was considerably in excess of the fifteen examined. In 1926 requests came for protection of cooked foods, wooden wheelbarrows, animal feeds, maize, agricultural produce, and salt; in 1927, cycles, smoking requisites, leather, and laces.[1] In cases formally investigated the commissioners collected evidence, presented in a quasi-judicial manner from proponents and opponents of each tariff; information on the industry, comparative wage costs and productivity; the impact of proposed tariffs on employment, investment, the Exchequer, prices and other industries. The procedure was similar to the British Safeguarding of Industry Act. Questions as to the nature of Irish industrial development were beyond their remit (Ferguson 1944, 40), and they were precluded from recommending any remedy other than a tariff, such as subsidies or industrial restructuring. Tariffs were generally requested to enable an industry to recapture the market share held in the recent past, frequently that held at the end of World War I. Leather output by 1926 was approximately one-eighth of its 1918 level (TC 1931, R 36/11 par. 59) and output of woolen fabrics was little more than 50% of its prewar level and only 40% of 1918 output (TC 1927, R 36/4 par. 33).

With the possible exception of the report on motor cars, the development of new industries did not arise, and even this application had a defensive purpose, as small coachbuilders sought to defend themselves against large manufacturers. At least two proposals were received for the establishment of a cement plant. One application lodged by Dr. Thomas McLaughlin, who masterminded the Shannon scheme, on behalf of a German cement manufacturer stopped short of a formal hearing because the promoters balked at having to disclose their intentions in public. A second, from a London firm of Porn and Dunwoody, representing a German firm who installed cement factory equipment, was dismissed on the grounds that the applicants were not "substantially representative of persons engaged in or proposing to engage in the production of cement in Saorstat Eireann" (F21/32/28). The need (publicly) to reveal detailed data on capital and costs acted as a disincentive to applicants wishing to establish

1. Based on an analysis of indexes in Finance.

new industries, while the requirement that applicants be representative of the industry was interpreted by Finance in a restrictive manner. An application by Dublin jewelry manufacturers for a tariff on jewelry, which had resulted from a joint employer-labor conference, led to detailed queries as to their representative nature before being referred to the commission, where it lay dormant (F21/21/28). The firms not associated with the application who received scrupulous consideration from Finance were retail jewelers whose interests lay in preventing protection. Fianna Fail T.D. Sean Lemass alleged that this clause was used to block applications from industries such as cycle manufacture and woodworking. In a letter written on Fianna Fail party notepaper, typed in a virulent shade of green, Lemass pointed out that many so-called manufacturers who opposed tariffs were primarily importers, and he urged that all applications from manufacturers be considered (F21/35/28).

The cautious attitude towards extending tariffs was reinforced by the opposition of industries, often beneficiaries of protection, that would be adversely affected. Opposition to tariffs was substantially more vocal during the twenties than after 1932 despite the greater volume of protection in the later period, possibly because the quasijudicial nature of the Tariff Commission gave it full vent. The application for a tariff on leather was restricted to harness leather because of opposition from (protected) shoe manufacturers (TC 1931, R 36/11). An application for a tariff on woolens led to protests from the Irish Merchant Tailors Association and the Irish Women Workers Union (F21/24/28) and hostile evidence from clothing manufacturers. Yet the judicial weighing of evidence did not prevent difficulties. A recommendation of a tariff on woolen and worsted fabrics priced in excess of 1s. 6d. per square yard faced early revision when clothing manufacturers, who were protected, complained that domestic producers could not provide an adequate supply of cheap cloth (TC 1929, R 36/44).

*Protected Industry: The Balance Sheet*

By 1929 the government claimed that 60% of nonagricultural imports were subject to tariffs, creating an extra 15,000 jobs; extending tariffs to remaining imports would produce a mere 10,000 extra jobs, "less than the number of emigrants in a single year" (*Economist,* 29 June 1929). The quoted figures were somewhat optimistic. Unpublished statistics for March 1929 (F21/31/30) indicate that employment in protected industries had increased from 8,695 full-time and 2,139 part-time workers to 20,643 workers; it peaked at 21,811 in March 1930 and then declined. The files document new firms manufacturing shoes, clothing, bedsteads, and corsetry; shirt factories established by Northern Irish suppliers; a "note of optimism" among manufacturers of sugar confectionery; and less short-time working. However, there was little growth in employment in soap factories because the Lever combine absorbed the duty and continued to supply most of the market from imports; few British shoe manufacturers opened Irish plants because they could still compete despite protection; while virtually all women's clothing save corsets was imported.

An unpublished 1931 report showed that tariffs on margarine, tobacco, soap, shirts, ties, blankets, and lower grade confectionery were deemed an unqualified success. Imports had fallen sharply, employment had increased, and competition, or, in the case of margarine, manufacturers' price guarantees, ensured that wholesale prices remained at British levels. The tobacco tariff, the result of Irish fiscal independence in 1923, proved the most successful. Employment rose from 500 to more than 2,300 by 1931, though employment might have increased irrespective of tariffs. The least effective duties were imposed by the commission. Rosary beads employment, which had expanded briefly from 53 to 160 (mainly women outworkers), stood at 93; imports were dominant and the consumer bore most of the duty. The tariff on down quilts yielded 5 extra jobs. Of the tariffs granted by the commission only margarine and woolens showed substantial employment gains, with margarine employment rising from 40 to 169 and employment in woolen textiles from 1,409 pretariff to a March 1930 peak of 1,883. Duties on motor cars and women's clothing were regarded as revenue tariffs. Cars were not manufactured in Ireland save in Cork, which was not dependent on protection, while five-sixths of footwear was still imported.

Tariffs proved less inflationary than had been feared because recession forced importers to absorb duties and because several protected industries, such as furniture, had sufficient internal competition. British and Irish boots sold at identical wholesale prices, though retailers apparently raised margins on Irish boots. In other industries the consumer bore part of the tariff, as did the exporter in the form of reduced profits. In the case of furniture, tariffed by the budget, domestic producers met 75% of the home market at a price somewhat higher than would have prevailed, while those buying imported furniture bore the full tariff. Imports of men's and boys' suits and coats amounted to £300,000 in a market of £1.3 million, but prices of Irish-produced suits were at U.K. levels, while importers such as Burton's absorbed part of the duty. One-half of the total supply of woolen piece goods was imported duty free, one-quarter was produced in Ireland at British wholesale prices, and the final quarter absorbed most of the duty. Protection brought modest but not insignificant gains in employment—overwhelmingly resulting from pre-1926 budgetary decisions rather than from the commission. The inflationary effect was limited because of depressed market conditions and because tariff levels never permitted domestic producers to gain a monopoly (McG Papers P36/b/28).

While the performance of the Tariff Commission aroused frustration among manufacturers, they appear to have been incapable of influencing the government. Their impotence was partly the result of organizational weaknesses: the Federation of Saorstat Industries collapsed, and efforts by the DIDA to become a national protectionist lobby by changing its name to the National Agricultural and Industrial Development Association (NAIDA) in 1929 proved ineffective. Its new constitution committed the organization to making the Irish economy "as self-contained as possible" "by means of representations to or co-operation with the Free State Government" (NAIDA 1905–1935, 30,33). However the similarity between the NAIDA's aims and the Fianna Fail program weakened its potential leverage and caused some members to fear that it had become "the shuttlecock of a political party" (NAIDA minutes 2 June 1930). The antitariff stance of Guinness, Jacobs and the Dublin Chamber of Commerce further weakened any protariff lobby, and despite resolutions demanding the abolition of the Tariff Commission, no sustained campaign for industrial protection can be identified. Agricultural interests proved considerably more influential.

*Agriculture and Self-sufficiency*

The agricultural debate was revived by the publication of a Tariff Commission report on protection for flour, which had been prompted by the dumping of British flour imports. Irish mills, which had supplied seven-ninths of the market in 1923—overwhelmingly from imported wheat—supplied four-ninths by 1927, and the number of mills had fallen from 80 in 1917 to 49 by 1920 and 32 by 1927, many working part-time. The request for protection was rejected in April 1928 on the grounds that the increased employment would not justify higher costs and that such a move would be a threat to biscuit exports. While this decision was unanimous, an addendum by the Industry and Commerce representative, Professor J. B. Whelehan, argued the merits of maintaining a domestic flour supply produced from native wheat and suggested that a tariff or a bounty on native wheat be considered in that context (TC 1928, R 36/3, add. par. xv). This was similar to the argument put by the Irish Farmers Protectionist Union, which represented farmers from mixed tillage areas. The publication of the report on flour sparked a series of resolutions urging assistance for Irish grain growing (*Cork Examiner* 23 May 1928; *Nation* 26 May 1928), and W. T. Cosgrave, who represented Cork, an area containing small mills and numerous tillage farmers, appears to have been responsive. The cabinet agreed that the ministers for finance, industry and commerce, and agriculture should consider Professor Whelehan's addendum, adding that "it may be anticipated that Deputy de Valera will return to the question again and will establish what progress has been made, the President would like therefore that the matter receive attention" (S2502). The cabinet also noted a Senate resolution favoring Irish wheat growing and the publication by the millers of a brochure arguing the case for protection. In July 1928, almost two months after they were requested to examine the matter, the ministers for finance, industry and commerce, and agriculture were again asked to report, but there is no evidence that they did so (Cab. C. 27 July 1928)—a common response by Cumann na nGaedheal to controversy.

The proposal to subsidize grain growing was resurrected by Fianna Fail under the umbrella of the Economic Committee, an all-party committee of the Dail established to consider economic prospects that was forced on Cosgrave in December 1928 during a debate on unemployment. At Fianna Fail insistence, the first topic considered was domestic wheat growing and protection for Irish flour. By April 1929 the committee had produced two polarized reports, with the government majority rejecting any subsidy or tariff (Economic Committee, report 1, 1929, par. 68) and the minority advocating measures to stimulate the supply of up to 50% of wheat from native sources. The opinions proved so irreconcilable that the committee was wound up in July 1929 (S5768).

Protectionist interests returned to the fray in the autumn of 1929 with an application from the Irish Grain Growers Association for an inquiry into the possibility of mixing home grown grain with imported maize for use in animal feed. The proposal was outside the remit of the Tariff Commission but the cabinet deemed them a tribunal with authority to consider the matter (Cab. C 4/109, 23 Oct. 1929). This decision gave rise to an arrogant response from McElligott, the commission's chairman, who undertook to serve on condition that the government realized that the commission's ordinary work would be delayed and that it could give no commitment on a completion date. Cosgrave replied, hoping for a report by the spring (S5439). However, the report rejecting the application did not appear until July 1931, and by that time the agricultural protection lobby had gained further momentum (Grain Inq. Tribunal, 1931, R. 44, 129). In October 1930 a conference of the Irish Grain Growers Association, attended by county councillors and Dail deputies passed resolutions favoring comprehensive agricultural protection. Their demands, forwarded to the cabinet in a letter signed by three deputies, representing Cumann na nGaedheal, Labour, and Fianna Fail, included a ban on the import of oats; a tribunal to determine the appropriate level of barley and malt imports for brewing, with a view to banning all other imports; duties on bacon and pork, with a total ban on imports within eighteen months; a ban on imports of eggs and dairy produce (S6081); and a butter tariff to finance the storage of summer butter (TC 1931, R 36/9).

*Reform of the Tariff Commission*

The proposal for a tariff on butter coupled with delays in obtaining a report from the Grain Inquiry Tribunal prompted Hogan in October 1930 to propose the establishment of a permanent Tariff Commission with full-time officials, a decision approved by the cabinet two weeks later (S6081). Whether the new commission was envisaged as more amenable to protectionist demands or simply as operating more speedily is unclear. Chaired by Henry O'Friel of the Department of Justice, the commission downgraded Finance and excluded Industry and Commerce (Cabinet Conclusions C5/24, 5/25; Cabinet Paper S4 950/2). This reorganization appears surprising until it is realized that the commission was constituted to deal with agriculture, a point emphasized by the minister for finance when he moved the legislation in the Dail (PDDE 27 Nov. 1930).

It is difficult to decide whether this move marks a fundamental change in government policy. Reports were issued within months rather than years, though not sufficiently promptly to meet changing economic conditions, and all five reports granted protection to butter, oats, bacon, linen piece goods, and some categories of leather (TC 1930, R 36/13, 1931, R 36/9–12). The report on linen piece goods (TC 1930, R 36/13) was described by McElligott, the previous chairman, as "the least valuable that has been made so far," and he suggested that the reports "should be examined before adoption and should certainly not be adopted as a matter of course" (Blythe Papers, P24/414), advice which was ignored. While the commission had been reconstituted to deal with a tariff on butter, the government argued that the application would lead to such a volume of forestalling imports that it was necessary to introduce an emergency tariff in anticipation of the report. This was done in November 1930, within two days of the application being lodged, which made the publication of a report in January 1931 recommending a tariff somewhat superfluous. However, the cabinet was not totally converted to the merits of wider protection. A recommendation that the duty-free threshold for imports of woolen cloths be lowered to compensate for falling textile prices (TC 1931, R 36/10) was initially approved by the cabinet; then second thoughts prevailed in the person of Patrick Hogan, who was absent from the meeting. It was the sole item discussed at a special cabinet meeting attended by Hogan and senior officials of Industry and Commerce at which it was decided that "no action should be taken on the matter pending further consideration." Although the tariff was approved (Cabinet Conclusions, 5/49, 24 Feb., C 5/50, 25 Feb., C. 5/51, 2 Mar. 1931), the delays suggest greater willingness to concede protection for agriculture than for industry.

By the autumn of 1931 a protectionist national government in Britain had introduced the Abnormal Importation (Custom Duties) Act, an antidumping measure permitting the imposition of temporary duties by executive order, that is, without recourse to the parliament. Weeks later in November 1931, the Cosgrave government passed virtually identical legislation, giving the executive power for a nine-month period to impose such duties as were deemed "immediately necessary to prevent an expected dumping of goods or other threatened industrial injury" (Ryan 1949, 54-56). Cumann na nGaedheal's willingness to embrace protection appears to have been a reaction to changing British policy and to the perceived impact of international depression on Irish agriculture. Irish national income estimates suggest a fall of 7% from 1929 to 1931, small by international standards though agriculture fell by over 12%. While allowing for price changes, real incomes rose by 2% between 1929 and 1931 (CBC 1938, 77–78), many Irish farmers experienced declining living standards. Exports fell by 10% in volume in 1931; agricultural prices fell more rapidly than other prices, while payments of land annuities or bank debts remained constant, and poorer farmers suffered from the decline in emigrants' remittances. The impact was intensified because it followed several years of poor agricultural performance. The Abnormal Importation Act offered little relief. A comparison of imports for the first five months of 1929, 1930, 1931, and 1932 suggests that "no actual dumping took place" (Ryan 1949, 61), though the quantity of agricultural imports rose marginally and prices fell. The problems of Irish agriculture lay not in dumping but in falling prices. Agriculture showed growing enthusiasm for protection, partly in imitation of British demands and as a device to boost prices and create new product options. While Cumann na nGaedheal responded to the pressure for agricultural tariffs, the government party was being forced to adopt positions similar to those long held by Fianna Fail.

*Cumann na nGaedheal Policy Towards Industry*

Cumann na nGaedheal's reluctance to embrace industrial protection was more deep-rooted than a mere distaste for tariffs and raised issues more complex than agricultural protection. The party saw the role of the state as furthering competition and market interests. When it intervened in establishing a state broadcasting system and a state electricity service it did so because it feared the alternative of a private monopoly (Manning and McDowell 1984, 65–67). This fear of monopolies or cartels and their power to control prices, coupled with a reluctance to become directly involved in industry, is a dominant feature of Cumann na nGaedheal and increased over time.

The 1920s were characterized by major shifts in industrial structure necessitating rationalization if some industries were to survive. In 1925 the government assisted the restructuring of the Dublin glass bottle industry by means of a tariff and finance from the trade loan guarantee scheme, which was used to refloat the Irish Glass Bottle Company. However, Brennan, as secretary of finance, referred the arrangements to the comptroller and auditor-general, and the initiative was not repeated (Daly 1984a, 81). The Dublin paper industry suffered major recession in the twenties that was intensified by a tariff on Irish exports to Britain and Northern Ireland.

Demands for protection in 1925 and 1926 were rejected by the interdepartmental committee, and on 19 October 1927 an application by a terminally ill industry was referred to the Tariff Commission. The Clondalkin mill closed shortly afterwards, and its reopening was dependent on protection. The mill was bought in 1928 by Dublin businessman David Frame, who attempted to resell it to Scottish-based paper consortia. Efforts to reopen it failed because interested parties claimed that protection was essential in order to raise working capital. The Tariff Commission resisted such threats and blandishments. Banner headlines in the *Irish Times,* a newspaper not accustomed to such a style, described Clondalkin as "The Village of Gloom"; deputations to the government from the Clondalkin Development Committee led by the parish priest and representations to W. T. Cosgrave from his former colleague J. J. Walsh were ineffectual. No report was forthcoming until October 1930—over three years after it was commissioned—and the application was rejected (TC 1930, R 36/7). The commission viewed the bargaining process involved in the sale of the mill with distaste, in particular the unwillingness of prospective purchasers to invest without an assurance of tariffs. Commissioners feared that a syndicate would purchase the mill, and having obtained protection, cash in their investment by floating a public company. They pointed out that no Irish mill was equipped to meet modern conditions and that considerable capital investment was required; however, they failed to recognize that such investment was unlikely without protection (F21/7/31).

Both ministers and officials appear uneasy in their dealings with industrialists and unwilling, even incapable, of taking a decision seen to favor one company over another or to bring financial benefits in its train. This reluctance to bargain with industry grew over time, reflecting an awareness of the financial implications of government decisions. In February 1922 Arthur Griffith, head of the provisional government, apparently gave the Ford company an assurance that free trade in motor cars and parts would continue between Britain and Ireland; Irish excise duties were altered in 1922 and again in 1926 to favor Ford vehicles (Jacobson 1977, 51–54). However, this agreement may have engendered a distaste for further dealings with foreign manufacturers, particularly as Ford was totally insensitive to Irish sovereignty, while the appearance of excessive profits being made by the firm who held the beet sugar monopoly acted as a deterrent against special arrangements of that nature. Such inhibitions may have influenced the fate of Irish flour milling.

Overcapacity in milling, which prompted the application for a tariff on flour, led to negotiations on reorganizing the industry between the Irish Flour Millers Association and Industry and Commerce, which offered assistance in the form of government intervention and credit. Government assistance was apparently predicated on a high level of efficiency and on price controls. McGilligan told the Senate "that in such a thing as breadstuffs we were not going to allow people to exploit the people's necessities" (PDSE 3 Dec. 1930). The precise details of the government's offer and the reasons for the failure of negotiations are unknown. Following the collapse of talks, Ranks, the British milling consortium, bought control of Irish flour milling and in 1931 reached a market-sharing agreement with the English Mutual Millers Association that divided the Irish market between British and Irish millers in the proportions that prevailed in the years 1926–1927, giving Irish producers a higher market share than they held in 1930. Producers were allocated a quota equal to their 1926–1927 output, and output was set at this level. While the agreement appears favorable to Irish milling, much of the quota was controlled by Ranks (Flour Milling 1965, A53/5 pars. 20–21), and public opinion held the government responsible for ceding control of a key industry. Official reluctance to countenance a flour-milling cartel led to the creation of a more powerful British-controlled cartel.

Fear of cartels or monopoly also delayed the establishment of a modern cement industry. The last small Irish producer closed in 1925 when the British Portland Cement Company bought and closed the plant at Drinagh County Wexford (CVO minutes, qs. 14004–5). While the major cement markets were dominated by cartels by the 1920s, Ireland because of its small size remained a free market, and imported cement from Britain and Belgium could be purchased for less than half the price charged in the country of manufacture. The industry was capital intensive, which would mean a monopoly producer, probably foreign owned, serving the Irish market. However, Irish cement consumption was rising rapidly from 95,000 tons in 1924 to 226,000 tons by 1931, the raw materials were readily available, and it seemed probable that the low prices would disappear when the British and Belgian cartels reached an agreement. Such considerations, plus pressure from Industry and Commerce officials and a battery of proposals from native and foreign interests, prompted McGilligan to circularize European cement manufacturers asking them to specify the conditions on which they would establish an Irish plant. The most promising proposal, from a Belgian concern, sought either a monopoly of domestic cement manufacture plus a tariff that would be virtually prohibitive, or a prohibitive tariff without monopoly powers, but offered price guarantees and undertook to provide capital. While officials in both Industry and Commerce and in Finance were enthusiastic, McGilligan feared that an agreement would be used by a cement combine to negotiate a market-sharing arrangement (TIM 91B Feb. 1931). His reluctance was decisive; a decision was deferred and then referred to a special commission. This move may have been an evasive tactic—Fianna Fail enquiries on taking office revealed that the commission never met.

Cumann na nGaedheal industrial and commercial policy is characterized by an unwillingness to make decisions during the government's latter years. When the party left office, in addition to cement, the restructuring of the insolvent Irish insurance industry— under investigation since 1926 (S4989, S2349)—a possible extension of the beet sugar industry, and a state scheme for industrial credit were also unresolved. Inactivity also extended to the Industrial Trust Company.

### The Industrial Trust Company

Two of the most sensitive economic issues concerned industrial finance and foreign investment in Ireland. The former brought the state into contact with the banking system; the latter involved difficult policy decisions. The 1926 Banking Commission, which accepted the need for a cooperative agricultural credit system, believed that there was no significant unsatisfied demand for long-term industrial credit, an opinion shared by the Department of Finance but not by Industry and Commerce officials (BC 1926, 3rd interim report; McG Papers P35/b/10). However, commissioners conceded that, owing to strains resulting from independence, there existed "for a brief period to come" a need for special credit facilities "for new or struggling industries which otherwise would not succeed in attaining a firm basis of operation," though they argued that such facilities should be provided not by government but by the Industrial Trust Company.

This body had been established with funds raised from the government, from Irish-American investors, and from the commercial banks—each providing £50,000—plus £13,000 from private Irish investors, to provide long-term finance for industry and to take over the funding of the trade loan guarantees in the face of a boycott by the banks. The volume of trade loans proved slight—only fifteen loans amounting to approximately £275,000 were approved between Jan. 1926 and August 1929; remaining resources were invested in

British and foreign shares—"a temporary measure," it was claimed, until sufficient debentures became available under the Trade Loans Act "or other fully secured and profitable opportunities for investment in Irish industrial enterprise present themselves." The company's report of December 1927 revealed £214,254 in advances in the Irish Free State and more than £250,000 invested outside the country. In November 1926 the company arranged to borrow up to £250,000 from the banks, securing the loan by trade loan guarantees. In practice the company financed trade loans by bank borrowings and devoted its capital to speculation on the London Stock Exchange. Applications for loans from Irish firms not in possession of a government guarantee were invariably refused (B Papers 26290).

Such practices aroused misgivings on the part of U.S. shareholders. One Boston investor, Sen. James J. Phelan, complained that the company was engaged in speculation rather than in pursuing the purpose for which it was founded, aiding Irish industrial development. In defense the chairman, Sen. James G. Douglas, argued that the company was inadequately capitalized and that stock market investment offered a means of generating funds. He also noted that loans to Irish industry not guaranteed by government carried excessive risks and that there were few profitable lending opportunities in Irish industry (Blythe Papers P24/475). Senator Phelan's concern was justified. A surviving list of investments suggests that many were highly speculative, and the company became insolvent following the 1929 stock market crash. When wound up in the early 30s 87% of its investments were in British or foreign securities, and only 13% in Ireland (B Papers 26290).

The collapse of the Industrial Trust Company had adverse consequences for Irish industrial banking. Senator Phelan noted the damage done to "the interests of the Irish Free State businessmen looking for additional capital support in this country in the future" (Blythe Papers P24/475). Phelan gave his correspondence with the Irish board to Defense Minister Desmond Fitzgerald who forwarded it to Blythe who ignored the matter, despite having nominated two of the company's five directors. While the demand for long-term capital for industry in the late twenties was slight, the government must be faulted for not exercising greater control over the company's reckless investment policy, if only to protect the long-term confidence of investors. The commercial banks were equally inactive; it was in their interests that the concept of state-funded industrial banking fail.

## Foreign Investment

The expansion of foreign-owned industry in the twenties resulted from changing market demand, in particular the growing importance of advertising, which led to the emergence of large conglomerates in consumer industries. Depressed market conditions led to foreign takeovers and rationalization in industries such as flour milling. While the Ford plant in Cork was the most prominent foreign investment, most conglomerates resulted from the takeover of established firms, though some tariffs such as that on margarine led foreign companies to build Irish plants to protect market shares. In unprotected industries such as cement, foreign control meant closure of Irish plants and the transfer of production overseas; in protected industries takeover meant continued manufacture in Ireland but the eclipse of Irish firms. By 1928 foreign tobacco firms (including those from Northern Ireland) employed 1,400 workers compared with 450 in native concerns; soap manufacture was dominated by the giant Lever Brothers, while 50% of confectionery output was controlled by outsiders such as Crosse and Blackwell, Clarnico Murray, and Rowntree Mackintosh.

In 1925, Major Crean, a Dublin soap manufacturer, made a vain attempt to have a resolution against foreign takeovers passed by the Dublin Industrial Development Association (DIDA minutes 11 Feb. 1925) By 1928, however, a special committee of the DIDA "put on record . . . that the unrestricted influx of foreign capital is by no means desirable." It noted "numerous instances" of "old-fashioned Irish industries" being "crushed" by foreign combines. The statement listed virtually every objection subsequently raised against foreign industry: foreign key executives, lack of commitment to exports, a tendency to sacrifice the Irish factory, and minimum taxes paid in Ireland and maximum profits to the parent company. It demanded preferential tax treatment for Irish-owned investments and suggested government restructuring similar to that carried out in the dairy industry to avert foreign takeovers. In 1929 the presidential address of Sean Milroy, T.D., Dublin sweet manufacturer, condemned the unrestricted takeover of Irish industry by foreigners as "nothing short of filching away the inheritance of the people, or national suicide" (DIDA/NAIDA minutes Dec. 1927, Dec. 1928, Sept. 1929).

Attitudes towards foreign investment among officials and ministers also appear to have become more hostile. In 1926 Industry and Commerce noted with apparent regret the failure of some British shoe manufacturers to open factories in Ireland in response to tariffs because they were able to compete successfully from Britain (F21/3/30). Two years later McElligott objected to overtures from British sugar manufacturers Tate and Lyle, who wished to set up an Irish operation, on the grounds that it would be giving a monopoly to outside interests, though his minister was noncommittal and decided to meet the company (F22/19/28).

In 1928 Barrington of Industry and Commerce listed the controls that other countries imposed on foreign business and documented the extent of foreign industrial investment in the Free State. He noted that there had been little new foreign investment in the previous twelve months and that this pattern would continue if no further tariffs were imposed, though in that event there was a danger that many new firms would pass into foreign control. While industrial development by outsiders would be "more satisfactory" than no industrial development, he argued that development by native firms should be "the ideal to strive for." Given the lack of an Irish industrial tradition he felt that well-managed foreign firms could transmit industrial skills to Irish workers, though many gave few management opportunities to the Irish. Barrington recommended intervention in cases where firms in protected industries were taken over by foreign concerns. In the case of the confectionery firm of Williams and Woods, taken over by the British firm Crosse and Blackwell, he claimed that the value of the firm had been doubled "by the simple fact of imposing protection." "By selling the concern the owners turned into cash for their own pockets the concession which they, in common with other firms in the industry were given by the State on national grounds." He recommended that such mergers be subject to ministerial approval, which would be given, "if at all," when a refund had been made amounting to the increase in the company's value attributable to protection. Barrington saw merit in requiring all new firms, native and foreign, to be licensed, though he admitted that this would present problems. This report, like others originating in Industry and Commerce, was never brought to the cabinet.

Failing the extension of protection, measures for controlling foreign industry lacked urgency, though the Ranks takeover of flour milling proved a sensitive issue. A memorandum from Industry and Commerce dated Nov. 1931 outlining a proposed extension of beet sugar manufacture assumed that any expansion would take place under "an Irish company financed from Irish sources and controlled accordingly from within the country" (McG Papers, P35/b/25a), though this would have required special legislation and perhaps the establishment of a state enterprise, strategies unwelcome to this government.

The apparent inertia of Cumann na nGaedheal in its later years reflects a certain equilibrium. Any extension of protection would involve the state in issues such as controlling foreign investment, investing in industry, or providing for industrial finance, all involving departures from the free-market policy that the government favored, though this was increasingly out of step with modern economic realities.

*Conclusion*

The drift to greater protection in the years 1929–1932 was in response to changing external circumstances and growing internal pressures from an aggressive opposition and increasingly vociferous interest groups. The government's responsiveness to pressures from agriculture shows the dominance of that sector. The reconstitution of the Tariff Commission, that body's later reports, and the emergency legislation of 1931 were all prompted by the needs of agriculture rather than those of industry, though these events had a major impact on industrial policy. In the early years of the state the dominant agricultural voice was that of the cattle farmer committed to free trade. By December 1931 protection of butter, bacon, and oats meant that agriculture's veto on tariffs was weakened, and the indus-

trial lobby for protection had been augmented by agricultural interests. Lobbyists for industrial protection were aware of the value of
agricultural support: the DIDA emphasized the common interests
of agriculture and industry and urged that both be jointly developed
by means of tariffs (DIDA minutes Dec. 1928), and this is reflected
in the organization's change of name in 1929 to the National Agricultural and Industrial Development Association.

The small but powerful free-trade industrial sector that had
been vocal in the early twenties became mute. Both Ford and Guinness
decided to serve the British market from England. Ford began to
build a large plant at Dagenham in Essex in 1928 (Jacobson 1977,
55), while Guinness decided to build a brewery near London; Jacobs
already had a British plant at Aintree. External conditions, notably
the emergence of a protectionist government in Britain, provided
further impetus towards change, as did the virtual cessation of
emigration in consequence of mass unemployment in Britain and the
United States.

By 1931 agricultural and industrial interests were largely in
harmony as Gordon Campbell had wished some years earlier, though
bastions of free trade remained in both sectors. The existence of
Fianna Fail, an alternative government, gave protectionists a focus
lacking in earlier years. Their electoral victory in 1932 marked the
transition from the free-trading beer, biscuits, cars, and cattle lobby
of the early Irish state towards an attempted realignment based on
smaller protected industries in alliance with protected, more tillage-
oriented agriculture.

The economic policy of Cumann na nGaedheal during this
decade shows remarkable fidelity to British practices. The vacilla-
tions in their tariff policy are similar to those of Baldwin's government in Britain. Both avoided commitment on a general tariff, both
occasionally gave way to protectionist interests, both were strongly
influenced by agricultural interests (Capie 1983; McGuire 1938).
The quasi-judicial procedure under the British Safeguarding of Industries Act is similar to the Tariff Commission, as is the disappoint-
ment of industrialists with the outcome (Lowe 1942, 79). Most
economic innovations—trade loans guarantees, sugar beet, state-
assisted agricultural credit, and improved marketing schemes—are
identical to measures introduced with greater or lesser success in
Britain (J. Brown 1987, 111; Whetham 1978, 165). While it is easy

to criticize Cumann na nGaedheal's performance, the achievement of solvency and fiscal stability in a difficult economic period, given the costs of civil war and repayments to Britain amounting to over 12% of the total budget, remains impressive. The volume of Irish exports in 1929 was not surpassed until 1960 (Kennedy, Giblin, and McHugh 1988, 178–81).

The darker side of the story is less quantifiable. The unemployment register declined as depression intensified because the numbers eligible for benefit fell as insured workers lost their entitlement after six months unemployment. Those never insured whose expectations of emigration were thwarted because of international depression remain uncounted. No serious effort was made until 1931 to tackle Dublin housing conditions, which were among the worst in Europe. Parsimony in public spending and lack of provision for the poor and unemployed were inevitable given parity with sterling and a relatively free trading relationship that condemned Ireland, along with Britain and Scandinavia, to a depressed 1920s (Broadberry 1984, 159–67).

Tariffs offered relief from depression and deflation while demonstrating the reality of independence. This is not to argue that they offered the ideal solution to Irish economic inadequacies. Surviving papers by Industry and Commerce officials such as Barrington and Campbell suggest an alternative program of currency devaluation that would have eased deflationary pressures and made Irish produce more competitive on both home and export markets, coupled with selective assistance in restructuring and marketing, plus aid for agriculture. The program outlined by Campbell was characterized by pragmatism and flexibility, close relations between the public service and economic interests, and a lack of dogmatism on the relative merits of protection and free trade. Such an approach, though with a greater commitment to free trade, has been regarded as the key factor in the post–World War II success of smaller European economies (Conybeare 1983, 449; Katzenstein, 1985). While this plan would have required the creation of new institutions, people of talent in both the public and private sectors, and a government prepared to withstand the pressures of conservative economic interests such as banks and possible opposition from Britain, had it been attempted, it might have preserved the Cumann na nGaedheal government while easing the political polarization of the period.

# 4 The Fianna Fail Economic Revolution

THE GENERAL ELECTION of February 1932 resulted in a minority Fianna Fail government kept in office with Labour party support. Fianna Fail was to remain in office until 1948. The election took place against a backdrop of increasing republican and left-wing violence. In response Cumann na nGaedheal introduced draconian public safety legislation, while deteriorating economic conditions led to a supplementary budget in the autumn of 1931 that increased taxes in an effort to stem a budgetary deficit (Fanning 1978, 212–14). In its election campaign Cumann na nGaedheal portrayed Fianna Fail as sympathetic to republican subversives, rejecting political and economic ties with Britain, favoring state control of agriculture and industry, and threatening individual ownership of land (Keogh 1983, 134–59). Fianna Fail countered by accusing its opponents of doing the behest of unionists and freemasons and by offering both reassurance and an alternative economic strategy. Fianna Fail viewed protest as a consequence of economic deprivation. In October 1931 De Valera told the Dail that "if men are hungry they will not be too particular about the ultimate principles of the organization they would join if that organization promises to give them bread," but he affirmed that private property remained a fundamental right and invoked catholic church authority (Moynihan 1980, 187).

The party's electoral appeal combined what Oliver McDonagh described as "a nice amalgam of nationalism and democracy" (1977, 109): (1) removal of the constraints on sovereignty in the 1921 treaty; (2) an end to the payment of land annuities to Britain, "a burden relatively heavier than the burden on Germany from war reparations"—in 1929 German reparations amounted to 12.4% of government spending, Irish to 18% (O'Hagan 1980, 19)—and a barrier to Irish economic recovery; (3) industrial development "to meet the needs of the community in manufactured goods"; (4) tariffs to curb imports, create employment, and maximize economic independence; (5) greater self-sufficiency in food; (6) elimination of waste and high salaries in the public service to provide frugal living and employment for all; and (7) the revival of Irish language and culture (Moynihan 1980, 190). Party policies combined the party's use of the green card (Fanning, *IT* 19 May 1976) with populist economic programs favoring the low paid at the expense of the rich, the small farmer rather than the rancher. Such policies, which offered the "nationalist, neo-orthodox" response to depression, were favored to varying degrees by most European countries during the thirties in reaction to the failure of the orthodox internationalist path of deflation (Gourevitch 1984, 126). Fianna Fail aimed at ending emigration, a matter given greater urgency because of mass unemployment in the United States and Britain. As a party it was acutely aware of the potential dangers of unemployment.

In September 1932 De Valera addressed the League of Nations about "impending economic collapse." He argued that the crisis would not be resolved by reopening "old channels of international trade," the solution favored by the larger economies, and suggested that the basis of production, distribution, finance, and credit was in need of overhaul (Moynihan 1980, 232). He showed no interest in rebuilding the old economic order, tending rather to distance himself from it. Such an attitude was common to states in the first flush of independence who believed that they could do better than older, wiser nations. In 1932 an editorial in a Turkish journal wrote that "in our opinion Turkey is not part of the world crisis but stands outside it" (Spuler 1959, 239). The apparent collapse of the modern industrial economy suggested that this was not the model for the future and engendered a certain schadenfreude in nineteenth-century economic also-rans such as Ireland.

Fianna Fail abandoned concepts such as comparative advantage in favor of self-sufficiency and a sharing of economic resources. Its manifesto promised to reduce public service salaries "to levels more in keeping with the means of the taxpayers and the frugal living that all sections of the community must be content with until every one who is able and willing to work is given a fair opportunity to earn his daily bread." De Valera's League of Nations speech made the provision of adequate food, clothing, and housing the primary objective of economic policy. The agenda was an amalgam of nationalist and quasi-socialist policies often stolen from the manifestos of left-wing republican organizations, tempered by Gaelic antiquarianism and Catholic social teaching as found in papal encyclicals such as *Rerum Novarum* or *Quadragesimo Anno*. From the latter the party derived the concept of an ethically based or normative economic model as opposed to the liberal market economy and the belief that an economy should be regulated to meet notions of distributive justice rather than of competitive efficiency (Cahill 1932).

The message of sacrifice and frugality suited the early 1930s, but it predated and transcended the specific problems of that time. It rested on the belief that Irish society valued a traditional frugal lifestyle that rejected the materialism of modern cosmopolitan culture (O Crualaoich 1983, 47–61). This dimension showed continuity with Cumann na nGaedheal, who had introduced film and literary censorship in an effort to exclude the modern world. Fianna Fail extended this Gaelic, Catholic cultural revolution to the economic sphere. Its program had coherence: more intense nationalism would mean reduced ties to Britain, greater self-sufficiency at home, both cultural and economic, and a renewed attachment to traditional values of frugality and sharing. This would provide a logical economic program for depressed times while reaffirming values perceived as both Irish and Catholic. The program would diminish the attractions of left-wing republicanism and socialism, while ensuring Labour party support in the Dail.

### *The Role of Government*

Such policies challenged the parsimony in government spending that had characterized Cumann na nGaedheal. The Department of Finance lost prestige; its minister, Sean MacEntee, was less influential than Sean Lemass, minister for industry and commerce, and was actually excluded from the Economic Committee of the cabinet. Despite commitments to curb government spending, Fianna Fail approved increased spending on roads and housing (Fanning 1978,

218). Government spending jumped from 24% of gross national product (GNP) in 1931 to 30.3% by 1933—the outcome of new programs and of a reduction in GNP—and averaged 30% for the remainder of the decade. Agricultural subsidies took 41.6% of the increase and 23.3% was spent on land redistribution, with the balance divided between increased payments on old age pensions, unemployment relief, housing, and sanitation (O'Hagan 1980, 23–24). Spending was funded by raising income taxes, revenue from tariffs, and withheld annuity payments. Heavy agricultural expenditure went to price supports to encourage tillage and to offset the impact of international depression and the economic war.[1] The new measures failed to wean Irish farming from its dependence on cattle. While tillage acreage showed an 11% increase in 1930–1936, it was only 2% above the 1930 level in 1939 (Meenan 1970, 99; Crotty 1966, 137–57). Agricultural employment fell from 648,575 in 1926 to 609,178 in 1936, when the government had hoped for an increase, while a letter in 1935 from a Fianna Fail Cumann in Inchigeela, West Cork, a community of small farmers, detailed the hardships they suffered as a result of paying higher prices for animal feedstuffs, sugar, and flour because of government policies and the poor prices received for young cattle, their staple cash product (S9636).

The 1932 manifesto contained the commitment "to make ourselves as independent of foreign imports as possible" but noted that "the people of Britain and ourselves are each others best customers. Our geographical position and other factors make it unlikely that the close trade relationship will rapidly change" (Moynihan 1980, 189–90). With the imposition of British penal tariffs in July 1932, a policy of minimizing economic contact held sway. The economic war showed that given the choice between economic and nationalist objectives, the latter took priority, at least for De Valera. Whether all who voted for Fianna Fail subscribed to this position is unclear. In

1. The economic war is the term given to the dispute that broke out in 1932 between Britain and the Irish Free State as a result of Ireland's unilateral reneging on certain clauses of the Anglo-Irish Treaty and the Irish refusal to continue making certain financial repayments to Britain. In retaliation the British government imposed punitive tariffs on Irish exports to Britain, and in turn the Irish government imposed further tariffs on some imports from Britain. The dispute was settled in 1938 (see chap. 8).

1932 much of Fianna Fail's attraction lay in its appearing to offer *both* greater independence and material advancement for the masses. Within the cabinet both MacEntee and Lemass were undoubtedly critical of the economic burden caused by the dispute. In November 1932 Lemass painted an apocalyptic account of impending economic crisis—as grave as in the famine year of 1847—and suggested a series of "revolutionary proposals" requiring "dictatorial powers" to meet it, or, alternatively, "postponing the Economic War until we are in a better position to fight it" (S6274). While the economic outcome proved less disastrous than Lemass had envisaged, imports of British coal, cement, iron and steel, machinery, and electrical goods, vital capital equipment for industry, bore punitive duties, and resources were diverted to alleviating the costs of a trade war.

The economic war was not the sole constraint imposed by noneconomic goals. The intense nationalism and xenophobia common to Ireland, as to many new states, brought restrictions on foreign investment (Kerwin 1959, 237; Spuler 1959, 277). Social objectives required an industrial program designed, however contradictorily, to preserve the rural character of the nation, a concern Ireland shared with fascist Italy (Ricossa 1976, 289, 305). In consequence, industries were directed to remote locations, while efforts were made to reserve employment for male workers. The goal of industrial development was modified by socioeconomic and nationalist criteria, which were occasionally of a contradictory nature. Ireland was not alone in this. Countries such as Italy, Turkey, and former members of the Turkish or Austro-Hungarian empires engaged in similar programs of economic development coupled with autarky, xenophobia, and the preservation of rural society. Economic ends were sacrificed for political objectives (Sarti 1971, 104).

*Industrial Policy*

The broad thrust of Fianna Fail's industrial policy was developed by Sean Lemass, minister for industry and commerce, a man who combined nationalism and pragmatism. In 1929 he noted that a commitment to Irish industrial development and population increase could only be justified by a belief in Irish nationalism: "If we were concerned only for the welfare of the old political unit known as the United Kingdom we would not deplore the decay of industry and loss of population here because they were more than counterbalanced by the growth of population and industry in the other island." He added that "the agitation for the protection of industries therefore is identical with the struggle for the preservation of our nationality." His program envisaged increased employment in tillage and industry, the establishment of an Irish capital market and the reinvestment within the state of funds invested abroad, and legislative controls on foreign ownership of industry. He believed that only "drastic methods" such as protection or subsidies would alter existing economic realities (Gallagher Papers MS 18339). Initially Lemass shared the xenophobia common to Fianna Fail, though there is no mention of frugality, while enthusiasm for the life-style of the western peasantry also appears muted, and he differed from his colleagues in the importance he attached to economic issues and in his appreciation of the obstacles to be surmounted. Consequently he sought authority in economic areas, which often conflicted with the practices of cabinet responsibility and parliamentary democracy. Many of his efforts to control industry were thwarted by colleagues, particularly when they involved Irish firms.

Despite these restrictions Lemass possessed an authority in industrial matters equaled only by de Valera's in foreign affairs. The broad directions of industrial policy were determined by Industry and Commerce, and the department was totally reponsible for tariffs. While schedules of tariffs or quotas were submitted to Finance, the cabinet, and the Dail for approval, they were not altered, and the protectionist aspect took precedence over revenue considerations, despite a plea from Finance in April 1932 that duties be kept "as low as possible" to generate revenue (S8167). Customs receipts rose from £8.257 million in 1931–1932 to £10.223 million in 1935–1936 when increasing use of quotas brought a drop in revenue and marked the triumph of industrial development over revenue requirements. Lemass personally determined all key aspects of industrial policy. Files are covered with his handwriting; memorandums to the cabinet frequently follow the precise line of argument that he outlined. Files were cleared rapidly—his notes generally bear either the date of the initial memorandum or that of the following day.

With Lemass as minister, Industry and Commerce moved from the periphery to the center of government policy. The enhanced status is seen in its move from Lord Edward Street to palatial purpose-built offices in Kildare Street, almost opposite Dail Eireann, the only government-owned offices built since independence. Before 1932 officials had bombarded McGilligan with proposals to little avail. Lemass claimed in later years that when he was appointed "the Department was rotting through inaction" (Farrell 1983, 33). In May 1932 the cabinet established an Industrial Development Branch charged with developing new and existing industries, with full powers over the trade loan guarantees (Fanning 1978, 219). Industry and Commerce Secretary Gordon Campbell had announced his resignation during the closing period of Cumann na nGaedheal's term of office. (As Lord Glenavy he was to become governor of the Bank of Ireland and a key figure in Irish financial circles). Cosgrave approached a senior Finance official, John Leydon, to replace him, but he declined until the offer was renewed by the incoming government. Leydon did not always agree with Lemass's policies and reputedly told him so when first offered the position (Farrell 1983, 34); but they proved an effective team, and his Finance experience proved invaluable in overcoming the objections of that department.

Fianna Fail's industrial program evolved into what is now termed a mixed economy. State-owned companies were established to handle beet sugar, industrial alcohol, peat, and industrial credit where social goals predominated over profitable possibilities. However, most development was carried out by private enterprise attracted by incentives such as tariffs, quotas, and credit facilities. While tariffs were available to all, licenses for duty-free imports or quotas, rights to hire foreign workers, and trade loan guarantees were discretionary and could be awarded or withheld to achieve specific goals, such as directing a factory to a particular town. Policy was implemented by a combination of carrots and sticks. Official control was not as total as Lemass would have wished: while foreign-owned firms could be subjected to ministerial diktat as to location, labor force, size, and type of output, authority over native firms was substantially less. However, R. C. Ferguson, assistant secretary in charge of the Trade and Industries Division, stated "that in fact few factories were set up without prior consultation with it [Industry and Commerce] or against its advice" (CVO evid, MS 940, Doc. 171a).

*Tariffs*

The number of tariffs rose sharply so that by 1936 over 1,900 were in operation. Whereas most tariffs under Cumann na nGaedheal protected existing industries, they now extended to items not manufactured within the state. Tariffs were now decided in private by Industry and Commerce, and once it became known that they would be readily granted for industrial expansion or development, applications multiplied. The new system offered the advantages of secrecy in the initial stages of negotiation, greater speed in decision making, and a bias in favor of protection. While the Tariff Commission remained in existence until 1938, its sole task was the comic-opera function of deciding whether to protect prayer books, a task completed in 1934. Initially the government operated under the Abnormal Importation (Custom Duties) Act of November 1931, which gave it powers to impose temporary duties without parliamentary approval. The outgoing government used these powers only once, but Fianna Fail imposed a total of nineteen orders between 19 March and 7 July 1932 covering an extensive range of agricultural and industrial products (Ryan 1949, 60), and the budget in May 1932 imposed a further forty-three duties, the majority increasing protection for industries such as textiles and shoes that had been tariffed under Cumann na nGaedheal (PDDE 11 May 1932).

In July 1932, with emergency legislation about to expire, and ostensibly to retaliate against the duties imposed by the British government, the Emergency Imposition of Duties Act extended the power to impose tariffs by order, and this act remained in operation until 1938. These tariffs were generally subjected to Dail ratification or modified in the subsequent finance act. In 1934 the Control of Imports Act gave the executive power to impose quotas in addition to, or in place of, tariffs (Ryan 1949, 77–83). The level of protection was substantially higher than under Cumann na nGaedheal. Ryan has calculated that in 1931 Irish tariffs (excluding revenue tariffs), accounted for an increase of 9% on import prices; by 1936 the figure was 36%, a calculation that excludes the effect of quotas.

By 1937 Irish tariffs were one-third higher than those in Britain and were exceeded only by those of Spain, Turkey, Germany, and Brazil, and there was an increasing tendency to include minimum specific duties on items such as clothing, in addition to ad valorem tariffs. Part of the higher tariff level was attributable to the economic war, though special duties applied to only a limited range of imports (*ITJ* Sept. 1932); its main impact was the exclusion of British goods from preferential rates, though in cases where virtually all imports originated in Britain, as with shoes, a new general rate was introduced, higher than the previous preferential rate but lower than the old general rate. The abolition of economic war duties in 1938 reduced Irish tariff levels by a mere 0.5% (Ryan 1948–1949, 123). The majority of tariffs were motivated by development, not by political retaliation.

Most tariffs were introduced without detailed examination of the potential impact on consumers or on other industries, action defended by Lemass on the grounds that he "preferred to take the risk of making mistakes in proceeding in the way we are proceeding than to take the risk of producing the same results that the late Government produced by inactivity." He operated on the assumption that industry needed protection and should get it, unlike the preceding government, which had regarded free trade as the norm (PDDE 8 June 1932). Tariffs were highest on fuel, farm products, and foods and lowest on metal products, which suggests that with the exception of coal, an economic war tariff, account was taken of the country's resource base. Most new tariffs in 1932 were placed on food, agricultural products, and farm equipment, though it might be argued that the latter tariffs reduced the benefits of incentives for tillage farming. Other tariffs increased protection for shoes, clothing, and fabrics, reflecting the government's fears, whether based in reality or not, of increased dumping as a result of recession. The duty on shoes was increased from 15% to 37.5% with a preferential rate of 25%. Other tariffs affected consumer items and building materials in an almost random manner. Subsequent years brought smaller numbers of tariffs and greater precision in their drafting, and they were more likely to affect prospective industries. There was a substantial increase in the descriptive detail concerning items covered or exempt, and licenses allowing duty-free imports were introduced. The first quotas were imposed in 1934.

The tariff and quota schedules submitted to the cabinet as part of the annual finance bill reveal the importance of such incentives to attract industry. The 1934 customs proposals recommended a duty of

40% on imports of boot lasts because a British firm proposed to set up a manufacturing plant "provided a reasonable margin of protection is afforded." While they "hoped" to supply their products at "about 10% over the British prices" they sought a higher tariff to avert dumping (S2920). A tariff of 100% on boot and shoe laces was proposed to support the establishment by Messrs. Jordan Ltd. of Leicester of a factory in Ennis expected to employ 200 workers. The grant of a trade loan guarantee was advanced as justification in this case, indicating the use of tariffs to protect government funds. The 1936 schedule proposed a tariff of 75% or a minimum of 2s. per article on imported clocks, clock cases, or wooden parts of clock cases because "a private limited company is about to be registered for the purpose of assembling clocks. Protective duties are essential to the success of this project." "Considerable employment" was promised (S7757). Tariffs were also crucial to raising capital. The 1938 proposals noted that the promoters of Irish Steel Company were anxious to be granted protection in the 1938 Finance Act in advance of their planned stock market issue (S 9755). The share prospectus for Irish Tanners not untypically quoted a letter from Industry and Commerce listing the tariffs and duty-free import licenses available to the company (*IT* 26 June 1934).

While employment creation was supposed to be a key consideration there is little evidence that tariffs were evaluated on that basis. Schedules reveal a lack of selectivity and suggest that the wishes of most applicants were granted. Scant consideration was given to whether the item's importance justified the administrative or human costs. Dentures and second-hand shoes were tariffed in 1934; the duty on horseshoes was increased from 33.3% to 50% because of imports valued at £1,954. Bicycle reflectors were subjected to a duty of 75%—with possible consequences for road safety—to create a maximum of ten to twelve jobs. In the case of wigs the proposal for a 30% duty announced that "a certain amount of employment is given in their preparation," which was "capable of expansion."

The tariff-setting process involved enormous administrative costs for both business and the public service. It was frequently necessary to grant licenses exempting firms from duties to prevent hardship. A total of 7,573 hundredweight of ice blocks valued at £1,234 were imported from Northern Ireland during 1934, resulting in a successful application for protection in 1935. However, licenses permitting duty-free ice imports were introduced "to relieve any hardship that might result." The Nenagh firm, Irish Aluminium, was granted a 50% tariff on all aluminium items but proved incapable of making the full range, and importers were forced to seek exempting licenses. The code of duties relating to clothing was revised in the 1937 budget because it had become excessively complicated, listing more than 200 separate items. The resulting simplification occupied four-and-one-half detailed pages of typescript and involved an increase in the ad valorem duty or the imposition of a minimum duty level on most items. Such detail could perhaps be justified by the industry's substantial employment and import substitution potential. However, the 1934 budget addressed the problem that some brush handles were escaping duties by masquerading as duty-free handles for chimney or sewer scrapers, by imposing a duty to cover the latter categories. Rosary beads, the first industry protected by the Tariff Commission, still recorded annual imports of £4,000–£5,000 in 1934, despite a 33.3% duty. A minimum duty of 2 pence per rosary was imposed to halt this deluge; however, in 1938 Dublin manufacturers Messrs. Mitchell alleged that rosaries of fifteen decades were being imported subject to the minimum duty and being subdivided into five-decade beads, while others imported continuous strings of beads duty-free for reassembly. A duty of 37.5% or 3.4 pence per decade, or length of ten beads, was imposed to meet this threat (S9755). Until the Anglo-Irish trade agreement in 1938 there was an inexorable tendency towards higher protection, with preferential rates removed, tariffs increased, and minimum nominal tariffs and of quotas introduced.

While in theory the government sought to encourage a high level of fabrication many firms did little more than nominal finishing or final processing. This defect is inherent in the structure of protective tariffs. Effective protection, which measures tariff levels in relation to value added, shows that for any given nominal tariff rate, the tariff is least effective when an industry is engaged in high value-added activities (McAleese 1971, 9). It is not possible to calculate effective rates of protection for the 1930s, but McAleese's calculations for 1964 show high rates in industries with low value added. Examples of low value added behind high tariffs undoubtedly existed during the 1930s. A Tipperary linoleum manufacturer was deemed by Industry and Commerce to be "playing at manufacture" behind a tariff of 40%, earning considerable profits and flouting undertakings on price (Inds. A. Room 303). A demand for higher protection on weighing scales because they were being undercut by imports led to the discovery that Irish scales were built in Britain, tested, adjusted, and then disassembled for shipping to Ireland for remanufacture (TID 1207/144). The 1932 package tax, which imposed a further duty on imported packages, bottles, boxes, cartons, or other containers in addition to duty on the contents, led to the establishment of many packaging operations employing low-paid female labor. This development allegedly benefited foreign manufacturers, as the stamp saying "Packed in the Irish Free State" attracted patriotic consumers (*Irish Industry,* Oct. 1933, Dec. 1933). One surviving file in Industry and Commerce contains empty packets of custard powder submitted by an aggrieved manufacturer who alleged that his sales to customers intent on buying Irish products had been ruined by an influx of Irish-packaged powders produced by well-known foreign firms (TID 1207). The package tax was singled out for special mention by the British delegation at the 1938 trade talks on the grounds that it gave rise to "considerable irritation in the U.K." Irish officials defended the tax because it generated substantial employment (BT 11/2833, 21 Jan. 1938).

The structure of tariffs, the package tax, high production costs, and the small size of the Irish market made it difficult to achieve integrated production, as opposed to mere assembly. Tariffs on completed radios were set at 50%, and those on components were increased in an effort to achieve a high level of fabrication. However in 1938 Mr. Digby of Pye (Ireland) Ltd. claimed that the high cost of Irish components meant that companies found it cheaper to import completed sets. Irish-made batteries cost 11s. compared with 4s. in England, cabinets 21s. as opposed to 9s. 9d. His Electro-Magnetic Industries (EMI) counterpart stated that companies who engaged in full assembly were at a disadvantage as against those who made cabinets and assembled imported parts (TID 1207/348). Pye and EMI may have been guilty of special pleading; larger multinational firms were particularly adept at justifying their cases for tariff increases.

*Quotas and Licenses*

Tariffs proved a blunt instrument for industrial policy, often failing to contain imports because importers absorbed the tariff or because of the poor quality of native goods. The shoe industry had been among the first beneficiaries of protection in 1924; in 1932 tariffs were raised from 15% to 25% and subsequently to 30%, but domestic output only accounted for 37% of the market in 1933. In 1935, the first full year of quotas, the domestic share increased to 71% and continued to rise (CVO evid. MS 937). Lemass favored quotas because they offered greater control and opened the possibility of bilateral trade agreements. In November 1932 he urged the establishment of a Board of External Trade controlled by his department in consultation with Agriculture, to handle exports and fix import quotas. The board would become the monopoly exporter of agricultural produce, assist in marketing other products, and negotiate bilateral trade agreements (S6274). These ambitious plans never came to fruition because of the opposition of other departments; however, quotas were introduced in 1934, and by 1939 a total of 37 quota orders had been applied.

Quotas provided a more precise instrument of industrial planning and a further opening for ministerial discretion with the establishment of a register of licensed importers who would be granted part of the quota (S2261). While tariffs proved sufficient to attract light industry, capital-intensive industries required more total protection. It is doubtful whether Dunlop would have invested in a rubber plant in the absence of quotas. They permitted the precise gearing of supply to market capacity, which was among the ideals of self-sufficiency and prevented the competition that might drive Irish firms to the wall.

*The Control of Manufactures Acts*

Quotas provided only a faint shadow of the powers that Lemass sought to exercise over industry. His proposed vehicle was to have been the control of manufactures bill, which was one of the first measures drafted after Fianna Fail came to power. While its ostensible purpose was to restrict foreign ownership of industry, Lemass sought to use it to control all industry, native and foreign. As initially drafted it required the licensing of all manufacturing companies. While those established before a certain date, whether native or foreign, would be automatically entitled to a license, all new firms would be licensed at ministerial discretion, and licenses could be made subject to certain conditions (Control of Manufactures Act temporary file 21 May 1932). While the cabinet supported controls over foreign business, it opposed the licensing of native concerns. The discussion was lengthy, with the cabinet sitting from 6:30 P M until after midnight, and the minutes record that the draft bill "did not meet with the approval of the Cabinet in so far as it applied to the licensing of existing businesses in the Free State, or owned by Companies, a majority of whose share capital is held by citizens of the Free State" (Cab. C 6/29, 23–24 Apr. 1932).

The bill was redrafted to exclude controls on Irish-owned business and was referred to a subcommittee, from which Lemass was pointedly excluded, that included Sen. Joseph Connolly, minister for posts and telegraphs, Lemass's main cabinet opponent (Farrell 1983, 36), and Education Minister Thomas Derrig, an upholder of Irish-Ireland principles. During the Senate debate on the bill, Connolly explained that the cabinet had considered several drafts until they felt that the measure eliminated any possiblity of injuring existing industries. The second "thorny subject," according to Connolly, was the "question of possible interference with any of our own nationals embarking upon business." He confirmed that the cabinet had dismissed the possibility of restricting entry into overcrowded industries (PDSE 22 July 1932), which was Lemass's main purpose in seeking universal licensing powers.

The 1932 Control of Manufactures Act imposed no restrictions on domestic industry; only companies without majority native shareholding were required to obtain a license which could be made subject to conditions concerning size and composition of output, labor force, and location. Lemass said this was "the barest minimum which any Government starting on a protective policy in a country like this would have to undertake" (PDDE 14 June 1932). He made a further attempt to gain control of key industries in the 1934 Control of Manufactures Act. Lobbyists on behalf of Irish industrialists sought stronger powers, including restrictions on existing foreign companies (Daly 1984b, 255–58).

The 1934 act required that a majority of all shares and two-thirds of ordinary shares be Irish-held and that a majority of directors, including the managing director, be Irish. While the act failed to satisfy the more extreme demands of native industrialists it marked a further attempt by Lemass to control Irish industry, with powers in part 3 to declare any commodity a reserved commodity, a decision that would require a prospective manufacturer, whether native or foreign, to obtain a license. This provision was used only once, in the establishment of Irish Sewing Cotton, a plant for the manufacture of cotton thread at Westport, though several proposals for reserved commodity orders were initiated but not confirmed (S7568, S8826). The failure to grant exclusive licenses, despite requests from prospective industrialists, reflected the hostility of Irish industry and an apparent division of opinion within the cabinet.

Most capital-intensive companies were established, not with the protection of a reserved commodity order, but with a less water-tight guarantee of exclusivity. The undertaking, which came to be known as the Dunlop formula, was devised to meet that company's desire to ensure that its substantial investment would not be jeopardized by a competitor. In a submission to the cabinet, Industry and Commerce stated that the Dunlop license under the Control of Manufactures Act would have attached "certain promises and undertakings not enforceable by law, but to which both parties will formally express their willingness to adhere." The most crucial was the provision that if Dunlop assented to a ministerial request to manufacture any rubber item within four months, the minister would only favor a competing firm to the extent to which market needs would not be met by Dunlop (S6560). The Salts textile firm received an undertaking that the government would not grant any other firm permission to comb wool without first giving them the option of refusal (S9250). These agreements offered the attraction of confidentiality, hence immunity from criticism. The cotton-spinning firm Gentex, which had a similar undertaking, was informed that "no reference is to be made, in the prospectus (for a share issue) to the Department or to communications from the Department without Departmental consent and no reference to promises to impose duties. Our practice was to confine the circulation of such a letter to the actual promoters or possibly to the underwriters" (Inds. A. Room 303).

Tariffs quotas and licenses could be augmented, when it was deemed desirable, by state-guaranteed loans or by the underwriting resources of the state-owned Industrial Credit Company. For key industries such as cement, further controls were used, and state enterprizes were established to process beet sugar and industrial alcohol. Two key questions arise: to what extent did these measures permit the government to determine the shape of Irish industry in the light of their social and national objectives? What was the response of political and community institutions to these policies? These questions will be examined in subsequent chapters.

# 5  A Self-sufficient Irish Industry?
## *Aspiration and Reality*

FIANNA FAIL hoped to substantially increase industrial employment by creating a self-sufficient industrial sector under native control. These ambitious objectives were set by inexperienced men lacking in technical expertise, consequently achievement fell short of aspirations while objectives often proved mutually contradictory.

### *Employment*

The growth of employment would appear to be the most evident benefit of the new industrial policy. According to the census of production, industrial employment (for categories covered see table 1) grew from 102,515 in 1926 to 153,888 in 1936 and 166,174 by 1938. The reality of such growth was disputed at the time, however, by former minister Patrick McGilligan (McG Papers P35/259); and in 1959 Garret Fitzgerald compared these figures with the more modest gains recorded by the population census (table 2) and suggested that they reflected better statistical coverage rather than a true increase in employment (Fitzgerald 1959, 146–47), an argument repeated by David Johnson (1985 29–30; Daly 1988, 71–75).

Efforts to reconcile the discrepancies between the production and population census figures (table 3) proved unavailing owing to the different methods of compilation. Even if we reject the growth rate shown in the production census as a statistical illusion in favor of the more modest figures shown in the population census (table 3),

TABLE 1

Industrial Employment, 1926–1938

| Year | Transportable Goods* | Building | Other† | Total |
|------|------|------|------|------|
| 1926 | 57,237 | 9,852 | 35,426 | 102,515 |
| 1929 | 65,162 | 11,754 | 31,599 | 108,515 |
| 1931 | 61,380 | 12,530 | 36,678 | 110,588 |
| 1936 | 94,708 | 18,207 | 40,973 | 153,888 |
| 1937 | 98,973 | 15,009 | 47,230 | 161,212 |
| 1938 | 98,444 | 19,548 | 48,182 | 166,174 |

*Source: Census of Production.*
*Includes manufacturing industry, mining, and quarrying.
†Includes categories such as laundries, dyeing, cleaning, gas, water and electricity,
    canals, docks, railways and transport, and various categories of local author-
    ity and government employment.

gains in industrial employment between 1926 and 1936 remain impressive. The population census (table 3) shows gains of almost 20,000 in manufacturing, over 19,000 extra jobs in the building sector, plus further gains in electricity, gas, and mining.

The totals in the population census mask changes in the composition of the work force; employers and own account workers declined while employee numbers rose (table 4). Many self-employed workers and small employers were engaged in casual insecure employment, often in servicing rather than manufacture. The decline of almost 2,000 in the number of women engaged in self-employed clothing manufacture suggests that the true growth in clothing employment was 10,000 rather than 8,000. We can therefore argue that the true employment growth in manufacturing industry, recorded by the population census, was approximately 22,000 (118,000 to 138,000 plus a net 2,000 extra clothing jobs).

Employment expanded in the building sector partly as a result of government financial support plus the impact of industrial development. Mining and quarrying grew in response to the building boom and the encouragement of minerals exploration, while the

TABLE 2

Industrial Employment, 1926 and 1936

| | 1926 | | 1936 | | % Gain | |
|---|---|---|---|---|---|---|
| Item | At work | Total | At Work | Total | At work | Total |
| Manufactures | 118,219 | 133,188 | 138,109 | 152,208 | 16.80 | 14.30 |
| Mining & quarries | 1,704 | 2,721 | 2,042 | 3,106 | 19.83 | 14.10 |
| Transportable goods* | 119,923 | 135,909 | 140,151 | 155,314 | 16.90 | 14.30 |
| Building | 36,456 | 50,027 | 55,746 | 77,822 | 52.96 | 54.16 |
| Gas & elec. | 2,462 | 2,864 | 4,828 | 5,540 | 96.10 | 93.40 |
| Ind. emp.† | 157,137 | 186,079 | 198,701 | 235,570 | 26.45 | 26.59 |

*Source: Census of Production.*
* Manufactures plus mining and quarrying.
† Manufactures plus building, gas and electricity.

doubling of employment in fuel and power reflects some spin-off from industrialization. Building, mining, gas, and electricity accounted for 22,000 extra jobs. The total growth in industrial employment in the decade 1926–1936 was of the order of 44,000.

A second area of controversy concerns the timing of this employment growth with critics alleging that much of the employment gains predated the coming to power of Fianna Fail in 1932. The only figures available for the years between 1926 and 1936 are those in the census of production given in table 2, which raise questions of reliability. The growth of 8,000 jobs between 1926 and 1931 is an overestimate: Industry and Commerce figures suggest that employment in protected industries grew by 5,300 between 1926 and 1929 (F.21/31/30) and by a further 800 by September 1931; employment probably fell in nonprotected industries. The alleged growth in building employment appears suspect, given that the 1926 figures exclude the Shannon scheme, the largest building contract in the state (*C. Prod.* 1929, viii). It seems probable, that if part of the employment growth reflects improved statistical coverage, as

TABLE 3

Industrial Employment, 1926–1936: Comparative Measurements

|      | Transportable Goods | | Building | |
|------|----------|----------|----------|----------|
|      | *C. Prod.* | *C. Pop.* | *C. Prod.* | *C. Pop.* |
| 1926 | 57,237 | 118,219 | 9,852 | 36,456 |
| 1936 | 94,708 | 138,109 | 18,207 | 55,764 |
| Gain | 37,471 (65.5%) | 19,890 (16.8%) | 8,355 (84.8%) | 19,308 (53.0%) |

*Note:* The figures are not directly comparable. The *Census of Production* data are collected from factories and workshops; the *Census of Population* figures are based on returns by individuals and include the self-employed and those engaged in minor repair operations.

Fitzgerald alleged, this factor was operating to a greater extent during the years 1926–1931 than in later years, as statistical coverage improved.

The decline in employment between 1929 and 1931, a period of economic depression, was undoubtedly greater than the census of production figures suggest; consequently the figures probably underestimate the level of employment growth after 1932, though part of that growth reflects cyclical recovery. Unpublished statistics in Finance suggest that by March 1937 there were 80,510 persons employed in 243 protected industries, compared with pre-tariff employment (no date specified) of 31,125. Employment in these industries stood at 54,083 in March 1933, a gain of over 26,000 occurred in the following three-and-one-half years (F.200/27/38), which is consistent with the census of production. It seems probable that up to 40,000 industrial jobs were generated in the years 1932–1936.

The percentage expansion merits comparison with the Russian Five-Year Plan of 1932–1937, when industrial employment rose by over a quarter (Johnson 1985, 29) and was achieved with less trauma. It also compares favorably with the decade 1961–1971, the most successful in recent Irish history, when employment in manufacturing industry grew by 41,000 and by 24,000 in building, an annual growth of less than 7,000 (Coniffe and Kennedy 1984, 11).

TABLE 4

Comparison of Composition of Work Force
in Manufacturing Industry, 1926–1936*

| Item | 1926 | 1936 | Difference |
| --- | --- | --- | --- |
| Employers | 5,957 | 3,653 | −2,304 |
| Relatives Assisting | 1,527 | 3,860 | 2,333 |
| Self-employed | 27,741 | 24,187 | −3,554 |
| Employees | 82,994 | 106,409 | 23,415 |
| Total | 118,219 | 138,109 | 19,890 |

*Source: Census of Population.*
* Transportable goods, excluding mining and quarrying.

This growth reversed almost a century of decline in manufacturing industry. Employment fell sharply from the famine to the First World War, and the decline resumed in the postwar years. The 1912 British production census recorded 66,693 workers employed in manufacturing in what became the Irish Free State. While these figures are known to be incomplete (*C. Prod.* 1929,iii, xxi) if they are *no more accurate* than the 1926 returns, they suggest a fall in manufacturing employment of over 8,000 between 1912 and 1926. Any greater inaccuracy in 1912 relative to 1926 would mean a greater decline. An employment peak occurred in 1937, however; and manufacturing employment fell in 1938 in reaction to the Anglo-Irish trade agreement. The employment potential of protection had been almost exhausted.

Employment fell in export industries such as brewing but rose in protected industries. The census of production and the census of population present almost identical lists of the top sectors in terms of employment growth: boots and shoes, clothing, paper and packaging, sugar, hosiery, metal, bricks, textiles, timber and furniture. The list of industries in decline is also identical: brewing; bread and biscuits, fertilizer and distilling. Expansion was concentrated in light industry and building-related sectors. If we include electricity, power, and cinema—all growing rapidly—the list is remarkably similar to that of industries that were expanding in Britain (Plummer

1937, 10). This parallel suggests that government measures merely captured for the domestic sector a pattern of market growth that would have occurred irrespective of protectionist policies.

Net output grew by 55% in the decade 1926–1936 and by 62.8% by 1938. All sectors showing major employment growth, with the exception of furniture, more than doubled output, and some achieved figures considerably in excess of this. Declines were limited to the drink industries. Gains in output per head were less spectacular; this figure rose at an annual rate of 0.02% between 1926 and 1938; for transportable goods it fell at an annual rate of 0.81%. However, the statistics are distorted by the decline in brewing, which accounted for 30.6% of net output and 7.5% of employment in 1926—a productivity level four times the industrial average. Excluding brewing and malting, Kennedy calculated that output per worker rose at an annual rate of 1.23% between 1926 and 1938 and at a rate of 0.77% for transportable goods industries (Kennedy 1971,41). These figures underestimate the gains in individual industries. Expansion was concentrated in labor-intensive sectors such as clothing whose productivity was one-tenth that in brewing.

The only exceptions to rising productivity were the drink industries; vehicles, where the highly efficient Ford plant contracted and small assembly plants expanded; and tobacco, which suffered a temporary decline as a result of the closure of the large Gallaher plant and the expansion of smaller firms. Productivity in hosiery, which was expanding rapidly, fell until 1931 and then rose sharply. All other sectors experienced rising productivity despite rapid expansion and an untrained workforce. A comparison of net output per person in 1936 with 1935 figures for Britain and Northern Ireland revealed that while Irish per capita output exceeded British levels only in bacon curing, bread and biscuits, brewing and malting, and sugar and sugar confectionery, net output per head exceeded Northern Ireland levels in fifteen of the nineteen industries that were broadly comparable.[1]

Agricultural employment fell by almost 40,000, continuing a long-term trend. While higher industrial costs did not help, the fall

1. *1936 Census of Production.* However, it is possible that high protected prices may artificially boost Irish productivity levels.

in output of 2.8% between 1929/30 and 1938/9 was primarily the result of structural trends, international depression, and the economic war rather than of industrial policy. Danish agricultural output was virtually static in the thirties, despite the signing of a favorable trade agreement with Britain (Jorberg and Krantz 1976, 401–2). The number of registered unemployed rose from 30,000 to 105,000 during 1932 and to over 220,000 by the autumn of 1934 (McG Papers P35/259), an increase concentrated in western counties. This rise was a consequence of the virtual cessation of emigration and of efforts to encourage people to register as unemployed. Registration was stimulated by relief schemes such as free beef, public works, and the dole. The minister responsible, Hugo Flinn, admitted in 1934 that "the register to-day is not a picture of the unemployment condition; it is not the total of men normally seeking paid employment who are unable to get paid employment" but a reflection of the poverty of western smallholders (PDDE 15 June 1934, 14 Nov. 1934).

The only estimates for Irish national income suggest virtual stagnation throughout the thirties; however, it has been argued that this is an underestimate (Neary and O'Grada 1986, 9). Kennedy, Giblin, and McHugh suggest an increase of "about 10% in real GNP from 1931–8" (1988, 54). While this figure is substantially lower than that for Britain the performance is respectable when compared with other primary-producing nations. The primary-producing countries that performed best were those that redistributed resources from agriculture to industry (C. Lee 1969, 148–55).

*Foreign Industrial Investment*

Employment growth was achieved in part at the expense of the commitment to industrialization under native control. In 1929 Lemass lamented the existence of an estimated 459 foreign companies within the state on the grounds that a substantial foreign presence would make it more difficult to "adopt measures designed to protect National interests" (GP MS18339). Yet caught between conflicting aims of maximum employment and a sophisticated industrial structure versus native control, the economic aims took precedence. Foreign firms offered the prospect of speedier industrialization, diversification into areas where native expertise was lacking, and higher quality. The interwar years brought a wave of British investment in parts of the empire such as Ireland in an effort to avert the consequences of protection. Some investors were large firms, such as Dunlop, but many were comparatively small firms (E. Jones 1986, 4, 17) that were vulnerable to losing the Irish market; some transferred total production. Those filling a market inadequately served by native firms were generally granted licenses. Several were licensed to manufacture women's clothing because imports remained high, and there was no evidence that Irish manufacturers could meet the need (TID 1207/322). Licenses were granted to three shoe companies to produce women's and children's shoes, which gave rise to outspoken criticism from native shoe producers that Lemass countered on the grounds that existing factories could not fill the market "no matter how rapidly they expanded" while the new firms would bring rapid growth in domestic supplies without damage to existing producers (PDDE 29 May 1934). By 1940 a total of 94 licenses had been granted, but 39 had been revoked, and some firms such as Irish Aluminium held several licenses for different products. Most foreign investment took the form of joint ventures or of the establishment of Irish subsidiaries, a circumstance that reflected the political and financial advantages apparent in native participation and the realities of Irish industry.

Aspiring Irish companies and local development committees sought to offset their shortcomings by bringing in foreign partners, as did companies who diversified production. The Portarlington firm of Irish Travel Goods was the outcome of a partnership between a local miller, Mr. Odlum, the Dublin textile firm of Ferrier Pollock, and a British expert in travel goods (Inds. A. Room 303). The Slane Manufacturing Company, which produced flour bags, was financed by the textile firms of Greenmount and Boyne, and Smyth and Company, and by the jute manufacturers, Goodbody, in association with a British businessman (TID 37/118). It frequently proved easier to attract a foreign company than to expand established Irish firms. Plans to revive the tanning industry by encouraging the expansion of the Limerick firm of O'Callaghan were dropped in favor of new companies with foreign participation (Inds. A. Room 303).

Outside expertise was of particular importance in the many parts of Ireland devoid of industrial tradition. Local development committees offered little other than enthusiasm and capital, and native companies lacked the high product status associated with foreign branded goods. Foreign firms could bring Irish workers to their parent plants for training and could supply supervisory and managerial staff. These factors led to many partnerships with foreign industrialists. In 1934 the Killarney footwear firm of R. Hilliard and Sons entered into an agreement with a Leicester company to produce ladies shoes under license (Press 1986,79). The Nenagh industrial development committee identified an English company willing to establish an aluminum plant and approached Industry and Commerce seeking protection and a license to operate under the Control of Manufactures Act (TID 1207/601). A committee in Kilkenny persuaded the British shoe firm of Padmore and Barnes to establish a plant (Ir. Ind. Yrbook. 1933). The official attitude to such overtures ranged from benign neutrality to active encouragement. When Waterford businessmen establishing an iron foundry asked whether there was any objection to their collaborating with a British company, they were told that any arrangement that would increase the prospects of success was welcome (TID 41/75).

Irish wholesalers and distributors for foreign goods frequently acted as midwives for new companies, introducing suppliers to the government or to individuals and development committees with capital. There were many backward linkages from distribution to manufacturing. The majority of motor assembly plants were initiated by former distributors.[2] In 1934 the Irish representative of an English iron foundry informed officials that his firm wished to establish an Irish plant with the majority of capital provided by Irish customers. An Englishman who had previously supplied the Irish market was a major investor in a tannery; he was introduced to officials by his Irish agent (TID 41/75 and 43/63).

Other ventures were the result of active promotion by Irish officials. Leading foreign firms or companies with substantial Irish sales were encouraged to set up an Irish plant or to lose access to the market. Pressure from the government and rumors of further tariff

2. I am grateful to David Jacobson for drawing my attention to this fact.

increases persuaded the chocolate manufacturer, Cadbury, to build an Irish plant in 1932 (E. Jones 1986, 109). The Dunlop rubber company was informed that if it did not invest in Ireland, a competitor would do so and would be given a monopoly (E. Jones 1986, 26). When thread manufacturer Coats Paton did not respond to overtures the cabinet gave Irish Sewing Cotton a monopoly license and sought to exclude Coats products (S2843). By the late 1930s Irish textiles were dominated by Salts woolen-spinning plant and Irish Worsted Mills, both English, and Gentex cotton spinners, a Belgian firm that was approached following the failure to recruit a British firm. At a time when official rhetoric urged breaking ties with Britain, new links were being forged.

While the recruitment of foreign firms marked a breach with official policy, it aroused little controversy where no domestic competitor existed. However, officials often supported an established foreign firm against a native concern. In 1933 while government officials were negotiating with the Ever-Ready Battery Company, a Waterford firm commenced manufacture of dry batteries. Lemass minuted that "it will, I think, be ill advised to turn down the application from the Ever Ready Co. until there is further information regarding Waterford." It emerged that the firm had commenced operations without applying for protection, leading one official to conclude that it showed little hope of success. Another battery plant opened in Ballina but closed "owing to crude methods of manufacture and laxity of management." This firm subsequently asked Industry and Commerce to provide it with an expert to advise on purchases of machinery and with a loan to manufacture face creams during slack periods in the battery business. Both firms failed and one can sympathize with the decision to favor a proven company such as Ever-Ready.

Similar considerations governed policy on radio assembly, one of the boom industries. By 1933 with a mere 31,000 licensed sets, one manufacturer described Ireland as "among the least radio-minded countries in Europe." Negotiations had opened with two leading firms, Murphy and Pye, when two Irish businessmen sought a trade loan guarantee for radio assembly. Officials believed that neither had any money and expressed "grave doubts whether any practical application will be submitted." Industry and Commerce secretary John Leydon decided that the department should not encourage any foreign enterprise that would compete with Pye or give direct assistance by way of a trade loan or otherwise to a native competitor. When Lemass informed Pye that no restrictions could be placed on Irish firms, the company replied that it was only concerned with foreign competition. Both Irish firms and foreigners were discouraged. A file relating to another approach noted that "we have other proposals for the manufacture of radio sets before us and [that] on the whole they look much more promising. Hold up" (TID 168/9 and 1207/430). The favoring of Pye over an unknown Irish company did not arouse opposition, perhaps because it was not publicly known. However, the establishment of Irish Worsted Mills and the Salts yarn plants led to outcry. The firms shared directors and Irish manufacturers feared that Salts would give priority in yarn supplies to Irish Worsted Mills. F. H. Dwyer of the Cork textile firm Sunbeam Wolsey alleged that officials had prevented him from establishing a spinning plant to produce yarn similar to Salts. However, in return they claimed that Irish manufacturers had adopted a dog-in-the-manger attitude to all inducements to open a spinning plant and had been warned that Lemass would turn to foreign firms if that stance continued (Inds. A. Room 303).

The Control of Manufactures Act prevented a foreign firm from competing directly with native manufacturers. However, this stricture was readily evaded by a variety of stratagems devised by Irish solicitors, notably Arthur Cox. Some schemes met with tacit official approval; others were regarded with disfavor. A subsidiary of a British food processing company whose annual Irish turnover was estimated at £200,000 had a capital of only £200; financing was provided by extended credit from the English parent, and purchasers were invoiced from England. The shares were juggled so that 100 preference shares and 7 A ordinary shares were Irish held, with English shareholders holding 3 A ordinary shares and 90 B ordinary shares. As only the A shares carried voting rights the company complied with the law, despite 93% of ordinary shares and profits resting in English hands. Industry and Commerce decided against legal action, perhaps because the firm's solicitor, Arthur Cox, claimed that the structure was "perfectly legal." However, Lemass determined to restrict firms that were "Saorstat in name only" with nominal capital and foreign sales organizations. The company's application to import duty-free machinery was refused as was its request for a tariff on canned fruit, and Lemass later vetoed its application for a license to broadcast a sponsored program on Radio Eireann (TID 1207/653). This company suffered ministerial retribution because it was operating in an area adequately served by domestic producers and because of its blatant defiance of official policy. No efforts were made to challenge its status in the courts or to close legal loopholes, as such moves might have exposed the contradictions in official policy.

While censuring the food-processing company's stratagem, Lemass, his officials, and the state-owned Industrial Credit Company connived at a similar share structure for Salts, also designed to evade the Control of Manufactures Act. All preference shares and a majority of the 75,000 A voting shares were Irish owned, though the majority of dividends accrued to the English parent through ownership of 125,000 B nonvoting shares. Yet whereas the food canners were treated like lepers, Salts received official encouragement, and its shares were underwritten by the state-owned Industrial Credit Company because it created a high-priority spinning plant and because its capital value was not artificially depressed. The majority of "foreign" companies operated similar schemes, with two-thirds of voting shares in Irish hands and foreign participation rewarded via royalties or nonvoting shares. Some Irish citizens may have acted as proxy shareholders for foreign interests. Such structures avoided the constraint of licenses and prevented companies from being challenged, while guaranteeing tax relief on dividends.

While Lemass and his officials showed little hesitation in favoring proven foreign firms, they sought to protect Irish firms from foreign competition. Licensed firms were prohibited from competing with Irish producers; licensed shoe firms were restricted to producing women and children's footwear, though it is claimed that this was not enforced (Press 1986, 81–82). Native firms were also protected by less formal means. When representatives of the cotton-spinning firm of Greenmount and Boyne expressed fears of competition from the Gentex plant, officials suggested that the firms should reach "an amicable arrangement to prevent overlapping of output" (Inds. A. Room 303). Native firms regarded as utterly inefficient were shielded against competition from newcomers. Despite one tannery's having a "past history" that would not "inspire confidence" and another's being described as "quite hopeless," a tannery investor was told that Lemass "was not prepared to encourage a proposition which involved the wiping out of one of the other tanneries" (TID 43/7320).

An application by Lysaght's, a Welsh steel firm (part of the Guest, Keen, and Nettlefold consortium), to establish a galvanizing plant in Cork was welcomed as providing competition for the excessive prices charged by Irish structural steel producers. However, Lemass noted that while there was no power to restrict the items manufactured if the government did not require a license, "we should have an understanding with them that they will not do the classes of goods the other firms are doing" (TID 94/49). Such restrictions may have been politically justified, as they stemmed complaints, but they removed a stimulus to efficiency.

Foreign firms speeded the development process and produced sophisticated products that were beyond the competence of Irish industry. They also seemed more amenable to government direction. Lemass's power to control native firms had been thwarted by the cabinet; foreign firms could be slotted into specialised market segments, giving greater precision to industrial planning. Although officials were unable to dissuade Senator John McEllin from producing heavy industrial boots, which were in oversupply (TID 1207/7), they could restrict the British-owned Dubarry Shoes to producing ladies' shoes (TID 15/145). On the other hand licensed companies were severely constrained in their activities. While one scholar has argued that officials turned a blind eye to these requirements (Press 1986, 82), files show restrictions that verged on bureaucratic harassment. Irish Aluminium was forced to seek a succession of licenses as they expanded their product range, as was Jordan, who bombarded Industry and Commerce with samples of bias binding and knicker elastic in an effort to diversify into these areas (TID 1207/601–2). A Northern Ireland joinery firm that set up a plant in Donegal suffered lengthy harassment over hiring a "foreign," Derry-born foreman, while another Northern Ireland firm was forced to submit endless samples before it was granted permission to import fabric. The constraints were such that both Jordan and Irish Aluminium became "Irish" firms.

The Control of Manufactures Act made it impossible to license firms in sectors that Irish manufactures could claim, however nominally, to be supplying. Instead Lemass encouraged the formation of companies with nominal majority Irish shareholding (TID 1207/63). The Belgian textile firm Gentex was told that it was the minister's policy to have an option under which foreign interests would be bought out after fifteen or twenty years. When Dunlop reported that it was considering establishing an Irish company, officials responded that "in their own interests it would be a judicious step to take" (Inds. A. Room 303; TID 1207/1178). This compromise recognized the lack of expertise in Irish business and saw foreign companies as having an educational function while allowing Irish business and investors to share in the fruits of industrial development as directors and chief executives. Foreign investors benefited from the native camouflage and reduced capital costs, which permitted British firms to overcome restrictions on capital exports and a lack of overseas flotations on the London market. Not all foreigners welcomed these arrangements. J. H. Woodington refused to set up a tannery unless he had total ownership. While the legislation did not prevent foreign investment, it may have acted as a practical and psychological deterrent.

Little is known of the relationship between Irish firms and foreign partners. While Irish plants benefited from technical assistance and from loans of working capital (Press 1986, 79), the relationship was also profitable for the parent. From 1934 to 1937 Fry-Cadbury (Ireland) Ltd. made a cumulative profit of £37,594 on total sales of £554,000 (Jones 1986, 111). On the other hand, the supply of patterns, trademarks, or semifinished goods posed particular problems in terms of price and of the Irish company's freedom to manoeuvre. In 1933, for example, one official noted a potential conflict of interest in the allocation of profits from the purchase and sale of goods between the Irish textile firm Sunbeam Wolsey and its British partner, Wolsey, which had a 49% holding (TID 1207/63). An investigation revealed that the high prices charged by Irish Tanners, Ltd. were a result of the price of crusts supplied by its English parent, which the Irish directors "with childish faith" had expected to get at cost (TID 43/63). Other firms were dependent on foreign trademarks and patents. Foreign producers of well-known branded goods assigned their trademark to an Irish manufacturer in return for royalties. The Federation of Irish Industries argued un-availingly that the capital value of a trademark should be counted as foreign capital and come within the scope of the Control of Manufactures Act (FII minutes 10 Sept. 1937). By the late 1930s, whether through licensed firms or subsidiaries or through the assignment of trademarks, most of Irish industry had a foreign presence. Flour milling was foreign dominated, as were motor assembly, rubber, and cement; more than one-third of shoe plants employing in excess of half the workforce were British owned, while textiles, tanning, clothing, chemicals, confectionery, and toiletries all contained significant foreign presence.

Given the depression of the thirties, access to the Irish market was attractive despite its size, and Industry and Commerce was able on occasion to choose between rival suitors, though many foreign firms were experienced negotiators: during the thirties Dunlop dealt with governments in India, South Africa, and Ireland; Lysaght's had negotiated with the Australian government over many years (Jones, 1986, 166–67). In consequence, the balance of experience favored foreign businesses who drove hard bargains. Cumann na nGaedheal received three virtually identical proposals for the establishment of a sugar beet factory, and although officials saw nothing sinister in that fact (S4128), collusion must be suspected. Most prospective companies, whether native or foreign, were asked the level of protection they required, and this was frequently granted. The Ever-Ready Battery Company requested a 50% tariff, a license for duty-free imports until the factory was built, plus an undertaking that no competitor be permitted to establish a rival plant for ten years. Lemass approved a 50% duty noting that "even if the full requirements are not being met the duty will do little harm" (TID 1207/166). Requests for monopoly were common; however, constraints on licenses meant that they could not be granted. Most firms settled for unpublished undertakings, which lacked legal standing though they appear to have been respected.

Foreign investment yielded benefits in terms of employment, technology, and "self-sufficiency," and its proliferation can be regarded as a triumph of pragmatism over ideology. Camouflaging its existence while officially opposing the concept was at least contradictory, if not dishonest.

*Self-sufficiency*

Self-sufficiency was a key Fianna Fail objective, close to De Valera's heart because it represented a rejection of the modern world. In 1933 he urged the women of Ireland to turn their backs on the fashions of Paris, London, and New York, dressing only in Irish tweeds and woolens until Irish cottons and silks became available (Moynihan 1980, 252). However, Irish consumers were less inclined to reject modern consumerism than De Valera might have wished. Smokers favored cigarettes made from Virginia tobaccos rather than from the stronger flavored Irish leaf, and firms such as Carroll and Players counteracted efforts to promote native tobacco by buying it, as the government required, but not using it (TID 11/23). In 1940 Finance urged an end to state support on the grounds that there was "no more case for continuing to encourage the cultivation of this crop than there would be for encouraging as a matter of industrial policy the production of a commodity for which there was not only no demand, but towards which there was positive antipathy" (S11692). Hats produced by the Galway factory were boycotted by commercial travelers, shopkeepers, and the women of Ireland (CVO evid, par. 18439).

Other ministers linked self-sufficiency with romantic or quasi-social goals. Turf development was pushed by Defense Minister Frank Aiken, described by one contemporary as "the last of the Sinn Feiners," a man who "would have been an alchemist" in another age (Andrews, 1982, 116–18). Lemass, the minister responsible, showed little interest. Aiken was concerned to promote rural employment, but the state-owned Turf Development Board established in 1934 rapidly moved from hand-won turf to mechanical harvesting of state-owned bogs. Turf output actually fell between the mid-twenties and the late thirties; falling production by individual farmers (Meenan 1970, 125–26) outweighed the combined output of the Turf Development Board and a private venture to produce peat briquettes. Self-sufficiency in fuel remained a pipe dream.

As a goal, self-sufficiency proved too all-embracing to achieve consensus between ministers or departments and was used as a means of boosting individual or departmental interests. The Department of Agriculture supported tobacco growing regardless of consumer demand, while Industry and Commerce championed the recalcitrant manufacturers (S11692). Positions were reversed on fertilizer where Industry and Commerce enthusiasm for a nitrogen plant was opposed by Agriculture, determined to safeguard farming interests (S7901A). The Department of Local Government opposed the establishment of a cement plant because of the possible impact on building costs (TIM 91B). Finance opposed most self-sufficiency proposals, regarding them exclusively in terms of revenue and borrowing.

For Lemass, self-sufficiency had a modernizing ring, carrying the prospect of developing resources and deepening the industrial structure. He favored a planned economy where domestic supplies supplemented by essential imports equaled total needs and where competition and overcapacity did not exist. This goal involved detailed estimates of the projected Irish market, which proved an overly-ambitious undertaking for the Irish public service. Considerable time was spent estimating the potential market for leather, calculations dependent on the projected growth of the shoe industry that proved totally inaccurate. In 1933 officials estimated that the Irish leather market would grow to 225,000 hides per annum from 90,000 in 1931, and new firms were sought to fill this gap; however, they were limited in output and restricted in their product range to prevent damage to established firms and oversupply. A 1935 file reviewing four proposed tannery investments noted that "if these four projects go ahead our total consumption of upper leather will be provided for." However, Vincent Crowley, a Dublin accountant and chair of Irish Tanners, claimed that total demand would be almost 300,000 hides and sought permission to expand output and produce wet hides. By 1936 even Crowley's estimate had been greatly exceeded, and Lemass remarked that if he had anticipated such a level of demand "vis-à-vis Portlaw production, he would have been tempted to try to plan another tannery elsewhere. It is however too late now, I am afraid." The inaccuracy of estimates is but one example of shortcomings in planning a self-sufficient economy. Most tanneries relied on imported leather, which proved the key to Lemass's control over the industry (Inds. A. Room 303). Planning by Industry and Commerce lacked long-term perspective. While Salts spinning mill was established to provide worsted yarns, it did no carding or combing and used no native wool, relying on imported tops. War left the country as vulnerable as it would have been had all cloth been imported, though this was later remedied by establishing carding and combing facilities (CVO par. 259).

In other instances self-sufficiency was achieved at a price deemed unacceptable by some cabinet members, and it involved the government in complexities of international business far removed from De Valera's isolationist vision. While Lemass was willing to concede monopoly powers or special legislation as the price of attracting strategic industries, his proposals frequently resulted in intracabinet disagreements. This is obvious in the case of cement, where Fianna Fail confronted the issue of an expensive capital-intensive project needing monopoly privileges that had paralyzed Patrick McGilligan. However, the government had given commitments to establish a cement industry, and the Ennis Chamber of Commerce reminded its local T.D., De Valera, of his obligations by forwarding a resolution requesting action on this matter (S6137A). The first proposal put to the cabinet in October 1932 from the Belgian combine Ciment Briqueteries Reunies (CBR) sought monopoly production rights with price guarantees, protection against imports, duty-free imports of machinery and raw materials, and low-cost electricity. The proposal was referred to a cabinet subcommittee; however, the minister for posts and telegraphs, Sen. Joseph Connolly, who was not a member, demanded limitations on import privileges and noted that under the Control of Manufactures Act Irish nationals could not be prevented from engaging in any enterprise. This intervention caused Connolly to be included on a new subcommittee which proposed a bill, approved by the cabinet, that excluded all the privileges sought by CBR (PDDE 17 Nov. 1932). The Belgian firm was unwilling to proceed in the absence of the original guarantees (TIM 91B, Box 55), and March 1933 marked a return to the policy of restrictive licensing of imports and production. These proposals (PDDE 4 May 1933) formed the basis of the 1933 Cement Act, which was viewed as a preliminary step towards finalizing agreement with a manufacturer. This process proved more time-consuming than anticipated. An agreement with CBR collapsed because of company reorganization, necessitating another round of negotiations (S6137A).

In subsequent proposals put forward by French, Belgian, German, Anglo-Danish, and Irish groups the government sought to strike a balance between its commitment to native control and having the (foreign) technical experts financially responsible. Ultimately Cement Ltd., a specially structured company, came into existence with Lemass acting as midwife (CVO evid. doc. 164). The Anglo-Danish company Smidth, which was part of the British combine Tunnel Cement, provided £100,000 in capital and technical expertise. Finding Irish shareholders proved time consuming, given capital requirements of £750,000. While cement was exempt from the Control of Manufactures Act, Lemass preferred a company with two-thirds of ordinary shares in Irish ownership, which would be eligible for tax concessions. Initially it appeared that Messrs. Duggan and McGrath of Irish Glass Bottle Company and Hospitals Trust would invest approximately £150,000, with the balance being raised by public subscription underwritten by the Industrial Credit Company (ICC). However, the deal fell through. According to the British principals, when it became known that the Hospitals Trust had rejected the proposal "it made it difficult, if not impossible, to get any other large undertaking in Eire to join us."

Smidth contacted Charles Tennant, the importer of Tunnel Cement, whose Irish subsidiary took a substantial shareholding. This arrangement aroused concern as officials suspected that Tennant was controlled by Tunnel Cement, though when John Leydon raised this point, he received a categorical denial. However a reexamination of the company's capital structure in 1939 revealed that it was acting as an Irish front for Tunnel Cement, which had lent it money to subscribe for almost fifty times the volume of shares that it actually held in Cement Ltd. (TIM 9/41). This was not known in 1938 when an agreement was signed granting the company a monopoly of cement manufacture and imports; the import monopoly was conceded in return for a commitment to accelerate self-sufficiency (PDDE 23 Mar. 1938). The company was subject to controls on prices, packing, quality, and employment, with government rights to inspect records and to revoke its license, but officials viewed the power to limit dividends as the major safeguard against profiteering (Inds. B Box 53).

The subsequent discovery of concealed foreign shareholding revealed many of the ideological contradictions in industrial policy. In response to a decidedly frosty statement from Lemass "that it was felt that some English companies were taking advantage, through some of their Irish connections of the facilities which had been granted and thereby preventing the natural development of Irish industries," the managing director of Tunnel Cement denied that he had tried to conceal the capital structure. He claimed that the ICC's share prospectus emphasized that Tunnel Cement and its friends had subscribed for half of the ordinary shares and argued that they would not have been prepared to invest in Cement Ltd. if that had been unacceptable, though he offered to reduce their holding to one-third of ordinary shares (TIM 9/41). Thus McGilligan's nightmare of a foreign monopoly came true despite efforts to avert it. However, critics commented favorably on the prices and quality of cement (CVO par. 498), while foreign control may have been a consequence of inadequacies in the Irish capital market rather than of cartel strategy.

Self-sufficiency in flour also entailed a foreign cartel with less technical justification than in the case of cement. Legislation passed in 1933 banned flour imports save under license; cereal prices were subsidized and millers required to use a specific proportion of native wheat, to be determined annually. A new market-sharing agreement was worked out with the Irish Flour Millers Association designed to arrest the trend towards foreign monopoly, to decentralize milling, and to ensure competition (CVO par. 257). Few of these aims were realized. The militant rhetoric of opposition soon cooled in office and the British combine Ranks retained control of Irish flour milling. The government was constrained because the Control of Manufactures Act prevented action against existing firms (S6045). Rank's Irish interests were ostensibly transfered to native control with the 1934 flotation of Ranks (Ireland) Ltd. with a nominal capital of £700,000, half in 6% preference shares, which were Irish held, and £350,000 in 1.4 million ordinary shares, of which 1.25m. remained with the parent company. The commitment to preserving smaller mills necessitated fixing prices at a level that would ensure those mills some profit, resulting in substantial profits to larger mills, which produced the majority of output. This was readily apparent to Irish investors. Ranks 5s. ordinary shares were issued at a minimum price of 15s., the £1 preference shares at 23s. (CVO par. 232). Ranks ordinary shares, 90% in foreign ownership, paid dividends of 26%–

29% throughout the thirties, and the shares of companies owning other large mills, such as Bolands and Barrow Milling, were similarly profitable. In 1936 when Irish mills had gained a monopoly of the domestic market, the Irish Flour Millers Association introduced quotas which ensured no surplus production, contrary to the 1933 act. This move was not challenged by the government, perhaps because it paid lip service to the survival of small mills by reducing all quotas pro rata (Flour and Bread Committee of Inquiry 1951, R.81 par. 35). The consumer was the loser, paying higher prices for bread and flour with a maximum of 27% native wheat (Report survey team flour milling industry 1964, A 53/5 para.27).

Other self-sufficiency proposals remained still born because of opposition on the part of foreign interests who controlled the Irish market, or because of Irish concern with native control. In December 1935 the cabinet was presented with separate proposals for an oil refinery from the Irish-American Oil Company, Irish Shell, Industrial Development Ltd., and Sinclair Refinery Company. Industry and Commerce's memorandum to the cabinet noted that "the attitude of the Shell Co. to the establishment of a refinery here has all along been one of opposition," and their estimate was regarded as having been submitted "mainly to deter the Minister from proceeding with his plan." Irish-American also preferred "that the position should remain as it was" but submitted what were regarded as "definite proposals," while Sinclair withdrew because of pressure from Shell. This left the Industrial Development Company, an Irish company associated with London and Thames Haven Oil Company that was independent of the oil combine. Industry and Commerce proposed entering an agreement with Industrial to establish a £1 million company that would supply most of the Irish market and export to Scandinavia. This would be financed by outside sources and require a Control of Manufactures license. The department proposed that a small refinery established at Hawbowline should have its output restricted to prevent its being taken over by the oil majors and used to drive the new company out of business and that Irish oil companies such as Munster Simms and Greenmount and Boyne should be guaranteed against competition.

Finance opposed the scheme on the grounds of an excessive fiscal burden on the Irish motorist and out of fear that the refinery's promoters "are capable of negotiating with us to the detriment of the Oil Combines while working hand in glove with the latter, [and] they are equally capable of double-crossing us and selling out to the oil combine when the deal is through." This objection appears to have been instrumental in causing the cabinet to reject the proposals (S6138A; Cab. C 9/279, 16 Dec. 1935). Finance objected to revised proposals because the proposed capital of £2 million was twice the necessary level, a pertinent point given that the agreement restricted the company to a 10% profit margin. Finance also suggested a minimum 25% Irish shareholding and a further 25% allocated to existing distributors "to secure their goodwill." Sean MacEntee, the finance minister, agreed that "we are entitled to ask for a share of the profits even from the 'external market', " an opinion shared by Thomas Derrig.

Lemass met these reservations by proposing a ministerial nominee on the board, a separation of export and domestic companies, a requirement that 45% of capital be held by Saorstat citizens, and a restriction of distribution to existing companies unless a satisfactory agreement was reached with the refinery (Cab. C 7/328 2 June 1936). These conditions plus ministerial involvement in the choice of directors led to friction with the promotors, and there was further pressure from Irish oil distributors (S9341). By 1937 Lemass feared that a share launch would fail and proposed postponing it until the refinery was built (S9342). The parent company then collapsed, and in June 1939 the cabinet was informed that there was no prospect of the refinery's being completed by the original promoters.

Industry and Commerce presented an alternative scheme with £1 million invested by Lonsdale Investment Trust, which held interests in other refineries, and the remaining £500,000 being advanced by the Industrial Credit Company. This proposal was bedeviled by uncertainty as to the future of the ICC in light of the report of the Banking Commission[3] and the deep-seated mistrust of other ministers in Industry and Commerce's dealings with the oil industry. The cabinet minutes (De Valera was apparently absent) record that "we strongly object to giving the Minister for Industry and Commerce authority to complete negotiations on the basis of the information at present before us."

3. See chap. 7.

Subsequent meetings brought two new proposals. British industrialist Lord Inverforth (formerly Sir Andrew Weir), who had held one-third of the capital of the old company, proposed to invest £1 million in completing the refinery on condition that the government secure the balance of £0.5 million via the ICC, and the oil combine made its first overture. Industry and Commerce favored Lord Inverforth and noted that he sought ICC involvement in order "to have an assurance of Government support"; Lemass doubted whether the oil combine "could be relied upon to develop and maintain an efficient refinery here." However, Finance was attracted to the combine's proposal because it provided all necessary capital, while the department felt that with "the exercise of a little judicious pressure" Lord Inverforth could be persuaded to subscribe the whole amount—their earlier concern with Irish participation had apparently vanished. The cabinet instructed Industry and Commerce to seek an agreement similar to that reached with London and Thames. Lord Inverforth pronounced himself willing to finance the whole scheme with a provision to sell up to 50% of shares at par to Irish investors; the oil majors offered a scheme costing £800,000 that lacked a cracking plant and was less a refinery than a blending plant.

Efforts to secure cabinet approval for the Inverforth scheme were thwarted by Finance, which on 23 August 1939—the eve of war—secured its referral to an interdepartmental committee on the grounds that although no government financial liability was involved, "government credit would be gravely damaged if there was a further failure to complete the scheme as proposed." On 5 September 1939 the government approved an arrangement with Inverforth similar to the original agreement, though the onset of war ensured its noncompletion, with grave damage not to government credit but to wartime fuel supplies (S6148A).

Negotiations on projects such as a refinery taxed the skills of politicians and officials while lack of expertise and a shortage of domestic investment funds left the country at the mercy of foreign business. The shortage of capital could have been overcome by establishing government companies, and this was successfully done in the case of sugar. The Carlow sugar plant, which supplied one-quarter of national needs by 1931, was foreign controlled and subsidized by duties on imported sugar. A proposal by Industry and Commerce in 1931 to build additional factories emphasized that they should be Irish owned and controlled, though the capital cost of £1.5 million was regarded as beyond the means of Irish investors (McG Papers P35/b/25a).

An interdepartmental committee established by Fianna Fail recommended four further factories, each costing £400,000, financed from private, ideally Irish resources, with government guarantees yielding "a fair and moderate return" of the order of 4–6 percent. The government recommended that no subsidy be provided and that the industry be financed by higher prices protected by customs duties (S4128). The cabinet made a commitment in principle to some government shareholding though there was disagreement over its extent. The draft bill introduced in 1933 provided that ordinary shares would be government held (S7067A), a majority of directors would be appointed by the minister for finance, and preference shares and government-guaranteed debentures would be sold to the public, an operation successfully carried out by the Industrial Credit Company (PDDE 21 July 1933). The establishment of three additional factories led to an increase in beet sugar acreage from 13,686 acres in 1932–1933 to a peak of 57,608 acres by 1936. By 1939 acreage had fallen to 41,661, and prices paid to growers proved higher than anticipated (Minister of Agriculture reports 1932–1933 to 1939–1940).

The Banking Commission criticized the protected sugar industry, comparing the 1936 Irish price of 25s. 5d., with 8s. per hundred weight for imported sugar (CBC 1938, add. 12). However, the domestic price included excise duties, transport, and distribution costs, whereas the import price was the duty-free landed cost; the actual subsidy was less than 15s. per hundred weight, which compared favorably with subsidies of 22s. 6d. to 24s. 6d. in the twenties. The industry's establishment under state ownership did not reflect an explicit ideological commitment; the wish for Irish control and moderate profits, a reaction to earlier experiences, plus the substantial sum involved made state investment almost inevitable. Disguised foreign ownership would have been the only alternative.

Further state investment that took place in turf and in industrial alcohol did not provide a magic solution. Finance was consistently opposed and kept the Industrial Credit Company short of cash.

State companies proved unduly pressured to meet social criteria at the expense of cost considerations and remained dependent on external companies for technical expertise.

In 1935 a Swiss company, Hydro-Nitro, proposed to erect a plant to produce synthetic nitrogen fertilizers at a capital cost of £300,000 with an estimated selling price close to existing rates. As the scheme seemed potentially profitable, the cabinet approved Lemass's suggestion to establish a state enterprise with foreign technical assistance, similar to the sugar company. However, the cost overruns incurred in industrial alcohol plants had led to concern over costs, and the interdepartmental committee appointed to examine the proposals sought alternative proposals from the British Imperial Chemicals Industries (ICI) as a benchmark against which to test the Hydro-Nitro scheme. ICI estimated costs at £1.17 million, almost eight times the Hydro-Nitro figures. The committee was impressed by the thorough nature of the ICI proposals and concluded that the Hydro-Nitro scheme was "heavily under-estimated," leading one official to question whether Hydro-Nitro had "doctored" estimates to obtain support. While available information does not permit an evaluation of relative costs, ICI held a virtual monopoly of the Irish market and was unwilling to erect an Irish plant because of over capacity at its Billingham plant. It was in ICI's interests to exaggerate the costs and to deter the Irish government. The Czech firm Skodawerk produced a third estimate of £889,000 in conjunction with Hydro-Nitro. However, the German invasion of Czechoslovakia prevented Czech currency exports, though Skoda was "more anxious than ever" to proceed.

By March 1939 the committee had not reported, and no progress had been made. The failure to establish a nitrogen plant proved detrimental to national needs during the war years when imported fertilizers proved unavailable. The project was stillborn as a result of a combination of external politics, disagreement between Agriculture and Industry and Commerce, the success of counterefforts by Imperial Chemicals Industry, and procrastination among civil servants. Efforts were made to extend its self-sufficiency character by requiring the use of Irish gypsum and peat fuel, which caused delays and threatened to weaken its financial viability (S7901A).

*Exports and Self-sufficiency*

Self-sufficiency failed to reduce import dependence. Irish-grown wheat supplied less than 30% of needs during peace time; the overwhelming majority of fuel continued to be imported, as was tobacco, iron and steel, machinery, and leather. The proportion of imported foodstuffs dropped sharply, as did the share of light consumer goods. Imports of wheat, nonfabricated wood and iron, machinery, and textiles rose. While these trends reflect the intermediate stage in development achieved by 1938, further reductions could only come with capital-intensive projects such as a steel mill, which would require substantial raw materials. The failure to stem imports coincided with a decline in exports resulting in an increased trade deficit.

From 1932 the terms of trade moved sharply against Ireland. By 1937 the import price index stood at 91.2 compared to 74.3 for exports (1930 = 100) (CBC 1938, 108). This decline is only partly a result of the economic war. Denmark's export prices, also predominantly agricultural, showed a similar decline (Jorberg and Krantz 1976, 400–402; Johansen 1987, 47–52). The Irish trade deficit fell from £20 million in 1926 to £11.8 million in 1930 and then worsened to reach a record deficit of £21.25 million in 1937, though it improved to £17.1 million in 1938. The 1926 deficit amounted to 19.5% of trade compared with 31.7% in 1937 and 26.1% in 1938. Although the total volume of British agricultural imports fell sharply in the thirties, Ireland's market share fell (Kennedy, Giblin, and McHugh 1988, 210–12). Industry was not immune. Drink exports were more than halved from £5.4 million in 1930 to £2.3 million in 1938; exports of vehicles fell from £2.7 million to £19,000; textiles, mostly wool, from £1.6 million in 1929 (£900,000 in 1930) to £776,000 by 1938; and apparel from £183,000 to £36,000.

Contracting international trade coupled with protectionist trends in other countries and instability in international currencies were factors. The major industrial exports, Guinness, Jacob, and Ford, switched production to English plants for a combination of economic and political reasons. In April 1932, before the Fianna Fail measures that would affect them were operative and before the economic war could have been envisaged, Jacobs announced that in the event of the

Irish Free State leaving the commonwealth the company would be forced to lay off 50% of its Dublin work force (*IT* 16 Apr. 1932). An examination by Industry and Commerce of industrial exports to Britain from 1929 to 1934 concluded that the effect of the economic war had been comparatively slight and that, with the exception of cotton, linen, and jute, woolen piece goods, and possibly biscuits and condensed milk, "no industrial exports of any real importance have been affected—except porter which is in a special category" (F93/1/41). However, Irish industrial exports were few even before 1932, and the protected industries showed little prospect of developing an export trade (CBC 1938, evid. q11812). Other exporting firms shifted to the domestic market. Goodbody's jute mill, which had exported 80% of its output, produced sacks for the Irish Sugar Company (*Ir. Ind. Yrbook.* 1932; Inds. A. Room 303).

While the plight of industrial exports was not ignored government reaction focused on agricultural exports, and the problem was generally viewed as attributable to the economic war. In July 1932 the cabinet voted a sum of £2 million to help exporters meet the problems posed by emergency duties and to assist in opening new export markets (S6315/2). In November 1932 Lemass proposed the establishment of a permanent board for external trade controlled by Industry and Commerce that would establish an international marketing organization. However, other interested parties, notably External Affairs and Agriculture, were unwilling to cede authority, and the sole outcome was the establishment of a trade section in the Department of External Affairs (S6414).

Lemass also proposed using import quotas as a leverage in bilateral trade deals, but Irish agricultural exports were not in popular demand, though the 1935 German-Irish trade agreement (S4825) resulted in an improved trade balance between the two countries. In 1937 Irish exports to Germany amounted in value to 58% of German exports to Ireland compared to less than 10% in 1931–1933 (*ITJ* Mar. 1938). All exports to Germany were agricultural; the principal Irish industrial exports to countries other than Britain consisted of linen goods to Australia valued at £330, woolen tissues to Canada valued at £940, jewelery to British East Africa valued at £500, and tins of biscuits to outposts of the empire (PDDE 7 Feb. 1934).

## Conclusion

The aspiration of a self-sufficient industrial sector under native control independent of international market forces was doomed to failure. Handicaps such as low incomes, a small market, lack of fuel and raw materials require little examination. The dual aims of self-sufficiency and native control proved contradictory. Requirements of capital, technology, and expertise made employment and self-sufficiency possible only at the cost of admitting foreign industrialists, and a small market led firms to seek monopoly privileges as the price of investing in Ireland. However, the granting of concessions to rich outsiders ran contrary to Fianna Fail's commitment to native control, frugal comfort, and opting out of modern capitalism. Lemass does not appear to have been unduly exercised by this contradiction and would appear to have viewed such compromises as a necessary price for creating employment and furthering industrial development, though he was keen to ensure that part of the benefit accrued to Irish investors.

Yet shareholders, even Irish shareholders, fitted uncomfortably with the vision of an egalitarian peasant society, and Lemass's pragmatism was not always shared by fellow ministers. Where quotas, tariffs, or licenses were decided at departmental level, no conflict ensued, and decisions were taken at a relatively rapid pace; where the issue required cabinet scrutiny or interdepartmental assent, discord and delay proved common. Industry and Commerce dealings on the oil refinery were regarded with profound mistrust, yet the suspicious Department of Finance, whose minister expressed "very grave doubts indeed as to whether in their present form the proposals are equitable to our people," was prepared to welcome an inferior refinery from the oil combine because it involved the state in no financial outlay. Some of the hostility was due to Lemass's efforts to gain excessive control, and colleagues also balked at the appearance of authoritarianism, particularly where it impinged on the actions of native firms.

In practice self-sufficiency would have required monopoly powers and a level of state control unacceptable to Irish society. Neither Lemass nor his critics debated whether these were too great a price to pay for "self-sufficiency," indeed whether an industrial drive as dependent on outside forces could merit the designation of "self-sufficient" in the first place.

# 6  The Political and Social Implications of an Irish Industrial Revolution

THE FIANNA FAIL ECONOMIC PROGRAM placed major strains on a cabinet, administrative, and parliamentary system derived from more laissez faire British practices. Scrutiny was reduced and established practices overridden as power passed to Lemass and his officials. The cabinet was limited to examining major projects, though it cannot be coincidental that discussion appears fuller during Lemass's absences when Thomas Derrig was acting minister. This lack of consultation reflects Lemass's style of work and his department's skill in restricting scrutiny by Finance. On many occasions under Cumann na nGaedheal, Finance defeated unpalatable proposals by delaying a response; in May 1932 to overcome this tactic, it was decided that ministers could bring matters to the cabinet without prior consideration by Finance if the latter failed to respond to proposals within a fortnight.

In November 1933 a subcommittee of ministers was established to report on ways of eliminating delays resulting from Finance's scrutiny (Fanning 1978, 218). Industry and Commerce proved adept at exploiting the Emergency Imposition of Duties Act, which was passed at the onset of the economic war, and they evoked a sense of emergency, even when unwarranted, to secure rapid cabinet confirmation of duties. The department frequently commissioned the parliamentary draftsman to draft a new order before referring the proposal to Finance, which could be left with only one day to respond. Such behavior caused Finance Secretary McElligott to protest that in respect of emergency import duties "the functions of this Department are being reduced to those of the Post Office." Emergency duties received little consideration in the Dail as they required no legislative confirmation if limited to eight months, while orders sent to the Dail could be accepted or rejected but not modified. Scrutiny of budgetary duties was equally lax, and there is not a single instance of Finance or the cabinet altering the schedules submitted by Industry and Commerce. Dail scrutiny was also limited given the volume of tariffs, and while Finance objected to Industry and Commerce's failure to inform it, the department supported this trend. One senior Finance official endorsed the tendency to impose duties by executive authority with reduced Dail scrutiny and suggested that the process be extended to cover all taxes (F22/50/33).

Ministers and officials displayed common cause in extending executive authority, evoking the sense of a country at war to further this end. De Valera told the Dail in April 1933 that the cabinet needed more time away from parliamentary duties to tackle national problems and suggested that the Dail should be given "say six months holidays to get that work done" (PDDE 7 Apr. 1933). Lemass kept details of his industrial policy secret, arguing the need for confidentiality, to the fury of opposition deputies, causing Fine Gael T.D. James Dillon to accuse him of acting as "prosecutor, judge and jury between himself and any individual citizen" (PDDE 21 Nov. 1937). The opposition's greatest criticism was reserved for ministerial control over the granting of import licenses or of licenses under the Control of Manufactures Act. Licensing was criticized because it enriched the beneficiaries, whose names were not disclosed. McGilligan claimed that tariffs and licenses "should mainly enrich the community and not individuals" (PDDE 19 June 1935) but did not specify how this could be achieved. Opposition deputies pressed for disclosure of the names of licensed foreign firms, and Lemass was forced to establish a public register in Industry and Commerce.

## Fine Gael and the Economy

Lack of information was a major plank of opposition criticism because the issue did not commit the party to totally opposing protection. Cumann na nGaedheal walked a sensitive path between criticizing government programs and avoiding accusations of free-trade sympathies or of lack of patriotism. The general election of January 1933 resulted in an overall majority for Fianna Fail, and Cumann na nGaedheal subsequently merged into a new party, Fine Gael, which included the Centre party and the neo-fascist Blueshirts (Fanning 1983, 114–15). Fine Gael attributed all economic ills to the economic war and believed that, as W. T. Cosgrave stated in 1934, successful industrial development was impossible where agriculture, "the main industry of the country, is not a success" (PDDE 17 July 1934). However, the party was not prepared to restore payment of land annuities (McMahon 1984, 70–71), and would have been unlikely to totally reverse protection. In 1937 James Dillon argued that Fine Gael "believed and still believe, that in the existing state of the world a moderate use of tariffs can be defended on empirical grounds" (PDDE 10 Nov. 1937). However, the party criticized the speed and scale of protection and its implications for government control, for inflation, and for inefficiency. In June 1932 McGilligan begged that Fianna Fail "should not speed the machine too fast and beyond what the factories can cater for" (PDDE 17 June 1932), while Dillon claimed that national self-sufficiency "means in the heel of the hunt, either social evils of the Moscow variety or social evils of the Berlin variety" (PDDE 23 Mar. 1938). Fine Gael believed that tariff increases should be balanced by reductions in other taxes, and McGilligan argued that had this been done "there might have been a chance that a tariff policy would not be made the subject of violent Party disputation" (PDDE 19 Oct. 1932).

Fine Gael was careful to avoid charges of being less nationalist than the government and tended to occupy the nationalist high ground on some issues. Alleged evasion of the Control of Manufactures Act and government licensing decisions proved valuable weapons in this purpose. Richard Mulcahy repeatedly asserted that "aliens are getting into new industries and undermining industries already established" and asked, "How many factories have been opened by persons with the names of Matz, Gaw, Lucks, Galette, Wigglesworth, Woodington?" (PDDE 24 May 1934). The names changed but the tenor remained the same: that foreigners were benefiting disproportionately from protection. Patrick McGilligan attacked the promoters of a razor-blade factory on the grounds that "one is a gentleman who came to this country from Palestine via Great Britain and the other is a man who came from Belfast via Tanderagee." He attributed this favoring of foreigners to Lemass's Huguenot blood, boasting that he himself was "a native Irishman without any tinge of foreign blood in me at all" (PDDE 12 Dec. 1934).

The opposition in the Dail exercised little influence on economic policy. Initially the Senate proved more effective because Fianna Fail was in a minority and because of the Senate practice of dissecting legislation. It passed a total of thirty-four amendments on the control of prices bill and more on the control of manufactures bill. Cosgrave was irritated by Senate thoroughness when he was in office, frequently cutting debating time and waiving rules (O'Sullivan 1940, 317, 198–201). It is not surprising that Fianna Fail restricted and abolished the Senate, replacing it with a more amenable body.

*Placating the Grass Roots: Industrial Decentralization*

While the legislature was given short shrift, Fianna Fail proved responsive to local interests. Most Irish towns sought a new factory or revival of an old industry, and local development committees mushroomed following the 1932 election. The public meeting called in Bray Town Hall in August 1932 to consider the town's industrial prospects was typical of many such occasions. Committees collected funds and, in theory, planned for industrial development. A Cork group prepared a pamphlet listing buildings suitable for factory use (Ir. Ind. Yrbook. 1933). These groups frequently evoked nationalism and memories of an economic golden age to generate enthusiasm. A meeting held in Hacketstown, County Carlow, in December 1933 was told that the town had once contained two tanneries, and amid deafening cheers a resolution was passed, which was seconded by Michael Barry, "brother of the boy martyr Kevin Barry," supporting the reestablishment of the industry (*Ir. Ind. Yrbook.* 1934). New Ross laid claim to a tannery on similar grounds of industrial tradition (Inds. A. Room 303, 43/2). Many committees proved successful at raising finance; those in Nenagh and Kilkenny identified a prospective investor. However, the majority did little more than collect money and lobby ministers and officials. The letter from Ennis to

De Valera seeking his support in establishing a cement factory is not untypical.

Lemass and his officials appear to have responded to such letters and met deputations, in contrast to the reluctance shown by Cumann na nGaedheal. This contrast is most evident on the question of beet sugar factories. Cumann na nGaedheal informed all pressure groups that the decision on location rested with the proprietors. The inter-departmental committee in 1933 urged to no avail that the location of factories "must be considered on economic grounds and on these alone, and that no other considerations of any kind whatever should be entertained if disastrous consequences are to be avoided." Deputations and letters multiplied and the cabinet devoted several meetings to considering possible sites (S4128). A wish for geographical spread caused cabinet numbers to choose Mallow, Thurles, and Tuam. At the Tuam sod-turning ceremony De Valera expressed the government's determination to spread the benefits and to ensure that the west would get "its share of whatever employment resulted from government action" (*IT* 25 Nov. 1933). The Leinster Beet Growers Association felt that they had been deprived by this decision and pressed for a fifth plant. However Agriculture opposed further dispersal on the grounds that "geography brought a factory to Tuam which has not yet proved a success" (S4128).

Fianna Fail was no less active in dictating the location of privately owned concerns. Few politicians were qualified to pronounce on arcane matters of tariff levels or of the degree of fabrication; the political dividends from a new factory were intelligible to all. Decentralization appeared to reconcile the paradoxes of preserving rural society while achieving industrial expansion. It offered political dividends, gave the impression that industrial employment was in the government's gift, and proved a major factor overriding antipathy to foreign industry. Whereas Irish concerns had local roots, foreign industries were footloose and could be directed to areas lacking indigenous enterprise.

The official wish was to spread industry as widely and thinly as possible with an apparent preference for maximizing distance from Dublin despite considerable unemployment there. Dunlop's wish to locate in Cork was accepted with reluctance. Lemass minuted that he had made unsuccessful efforts to divert the company, adding that "a refusal to agree to either Dublin or Cork would jeopardise the scheme" (S6560A). A potential tannery investor who informed officials that he had decided to locate in Bray was informed that "the farther he decided to go from the city the greater attraction would he lend to his proposal" (TID 43/63).

Decisions on location were determined with scant respect for economics. Building suppliers Brooks Thomas were urged to set up a plant in Bandon, County Cork, despite the firm's opinion that it "would be an impossible centre" involving substantially higher costs (TID 1207/171). A Welsh-based tannery who wished to locate in Drogheda, close to several shoe firms, was informed that the minister would prefer and might make it a condition that another site be chosen. The tannery was directed to Tralee, Sligo, New Ross, and Portlaw, opting for Portlaw on condition that the state drain a disused canal. Despite the cost, this decision was greeted with delight because it involved reopening the Malcolmson cotton plant, which had been closed for over fifty years, providing a concrete expression of industrial regeneration. A normally prosaic official minuted, "My own feeling is that there is such an attraction in having this old site occupied and employment given in the district that it would be worth while meeting this part of the application. We have had many deputations from Portlaw district" (Inds. A.Room 303).

J. H. Woodington was refused permission to build a tannery adjacent to his Drogheda shoe plant or in an adjoining town. He was informed that the minister preferred a town that did not have an industry and was dispatched to Mountmellick following local representations, despite the lack of a suitable site. When he turned his attention to Portlaoise because of an offer of local capital, officials proposed Tralee, "where all the capital necessary would be available." When he demurred because of distribution difficulties, Lemass informed him that a competing tannery was being established in Passage West and "that it is improbable that any facilities would be granted for the establishment of a similar tannery at Maryboro" (Portlaoise). Ultimately the Woodington tannery was located in the old workhouse at Gorey, replacing a proposal that had fallen through. Mountmellick and Portlaoise protested. Mountmellick was provided with a bag factory that employed females but responded with a

TABLE 5

Employment in Manufacturing, 1926 and 1936

| Location | 1926 | | 1936 | | Gain | |
|---|---|---|---|---|---|---|
| | No. | % | No. | % | No. | % |
| Dublin City & Co. | 42,082 | 35.6 | 55,105 | 39.9 | 13,023 | 65.5 |
| Rest of Leinster | 22,261 | 18.8 | 26,736 | 19.3 | 4,475 | 22.5 |
| Cork, Limerick & Waterford cities | 12,394 | 10.5 | 14,158 | 10.2 | 1,764 | 8.9 |
| Rest of Munster | 24,460 | 20.7 | 24,607 | 17.8 | 147 | 0.7 |
| Connacht | 9,165 | 7.8 | 9,513 | 6.9 | 348 | 1.7 |
| Ulster | 7,857 | 6.6 | 7,990 | 5.8 | 133 | 0.7 |
| Total | 118,219 | 100.0 | 138,109 | 100.0 | 19,890 | 100.0 |

*Source: Census of Population.*

protest mission and the threat, in the teeth of ministerial opposition, to set up a suitcase plant (presumably employing men), competing with a plant that they felt had been unfairly allocated to the adjacent town of Portarlington (Inds. A.Room 303; TID 43/75). Portlaoise became the location of Irish Worsted Mills.

Despite these efforts, the 1936 population census revealed that gains in manufacturing employment were concentrated in the Dublin area and Leinster. Munster, outside Cork, Limerick and Waterford, gained 147 jobs; Connacht and Ulster gained 348 and 133 jobs respectively (see table 5). This situation was undesirable given Fianna Fail's electoral support in the west and the aura attached to the area. Industrialists were prepared to locate in the midlands and southeast but not west of the Shannon or in border counties, except Louth. An exclusive manufacturing license was granted to Irish Sewing Cotton "because the Minister of the day wished to get employment in Westport," County Mayo (CVO evid. par. 14885).

In theory Lemass could dictate location to firms needing a license and could use tariffs and quotas, trade loan guarantees, or duty-free licenses to influence others. Such efforts resulted in hard bargaining that generally led to a compromise. The textile firms Gentex, Salts, and Irish Worsted Mills were directed to the west, all to no avail. Lemass was "disposed to press Sligo" or "a western port" as the location for the Gentex plant, dangling a reserved commodity license as a bait. When Father Kelly, a Longford priest, attempted to lobby for this plant, he was told that "although Longford was not west of the Shannon the Assistant Secretary thought there was a chance of a visit" (Inds. A.R. 303). Gentex located at Athlone on the *east* bank of the Shannon. Lemass ordered Irish Worsted Mills to inspect sites in Cork, Kerry, Cavan, Donegal, Mayo, Roscommon, and Sligo, but Dublin accountant Vincent Crowley explained that only Naas, County Kildare, could provide satisfactory water, labor, and market access. Crowley pressed his case "with some heat" but was informed that "the Minister would rather abandon the whole scheme and make arrangements with some other group than approve Naas (TID 19/145). The company's compromise suggestion of Portlaoise was accepted because of the need to placate that town over the loss of a tannery.

The associated firm Salts was anxious to locate close to Portlaoise in the interests of efficiency. However, the acting minister, Thomas Derrig, informed John Leydon "that every effort should be made to have the factory located at Ballina," though he subsequently compromised on any town west of the Shannon. When Vincent Crowley opted for the western town of Ballinasloe this was rejected, because it was earmarked for the Dubarry shoe plant, which had been forbidden to locate in Dublin. A mutual game of bluff ensued with one official reporting that insistence on a western location "means that we shall lose the industry altogether," while Mr. Crowley was informed that approval would be conditional on this. In the meantime a midlands businessman and local Fianna Fail T.D.'s lobbied on behalf of Tullamore. Salts expressed willingness to locate in Templemore, Tullamore, "or any town approximately the same distance from Dublin," and Tullamore was approved (Inds. A.Room 303).

The most extreme cases of decentralization involved efforts to locate industry in remote Irish-speaking areas where official policy sought to retain traditional language and life-style. In 1937 the Gaeltacht subcommittee of the cabinet, chaired by Derrig, sought to have several new industries such as the Gentex spinning plant and a pottery (subsequently based at Arklow) reserved for Gaeltacht areas and wished to promote other industries in competition with existing plants. These plans, which posed a direct challenge to the authority of Industry and Commerce, were sabotaged by a joint effort with Finance, and Derrig sought to bypass both departments by bringing projects direct to the cabinet. Lemass, who viewed the Gaeltacht problem "as solely an economic problem arising from considerable congestion of population," proposed that younger workers be encouraged to migrate for training and employment. While Derrig's proposal was rejected, the cabinet agreed that Gaeltacht plants should be given preference in government contracts, despite higher costs (S9164).

Decentralization added a further layer of distortion and affirmed the primacy of political and social aims. Production at the Jordan plant, located at Ennis on official instructions, was delayed for three months because of lack of housing for workers and was subsequently hampered by lack of water (TID 1207/602). A Northern Ireland joinery firm forced to locate in Letterkenny under the terms of its license discovered that all joiners were fully employed on housing schemes and was forced to recruit workers from a distance at considerable cost (TID 1207/26). These directives raised production costs and permitted companies to extract compensating concessions. The difficulty of attracting industry to Galway led Lemass to "compel" a hat factory to locate there, with the added attraction that it would employ Gaeltacht workers. R. C. Ferguson explained that "in consequence of this he was simply bound to support it," although the hats led to "something approaching a revolt . . . among the consumers" (CVO evid. par. 14839). The Dubarry shoe company demanded a trade loans guarantee plus licenses to import shoe leather and components duty free in recompense for being sent to Ballinasloe. While licenses for components were invariably refused, a civil servant minuted that "the circumstances of this particular factory being established in Ballinasloe might however justify a change in policy," though Lemass vetoed this concession. A deputation from the town in June 1938, prompted by the firm's difficulties, claimed that it merited special treatment by virtue of location, and officials arranged for the company to manufacture shoes under license from a Bristol firm (TID 1545).

TABLE 6

Decentralization of Industry: Employment and Net Output
*(in percentage)*

| Location | Employment | | | | Output | | | |
|---|---|---|---|---|---|---|---|---|
| | 1931 | 1936 | 1938 | 1944 | 1931 | 1936 | 1938 | 1944 |
| Dublin Co. B* | 42 | 43 | 43 | 42 | 59 | 53 | 54 | 52 |
| Rest of Leinster | 18 | 19 | 19 | 20 | 12 | 15 | 16 | 17 |
| Cork City | 7 | 8 | 7 | 8 | 10 | 9 | 9 | 8 |
| Limerick City | 3 | 3 | 3 | 3 | 3 | 3 | 3 | 3 |
| Waterford City | 2 | 2 | 2 | 1 | 2 | 2 | 2 | 2 |
| Rest of Munster | 16 | 14 | 13 | 15 | 9 | 10 | 9 | 11 |
| Connacht | 7 | 6 | 8 | 7 | 3 | 4 | 4 | 5 |
| Ulster | 5 | 5 | 5 | 5 | 2 | 2 | 3 | 3 |

*Source: Census of Production 1936, xxv; 1938–1944, xiii.*
* The drop in the percentage of net output produced in Dublin is atttributable to a decline in production at Guinness's brewery.

The more intensive drive for decentralization in the late thirties appears to have been ineffective (see table 6). Rural areas gained little: as consumers they were net losers. Western areas dominated by small farmers were net losers from programs to grow wheat, sugar, and animal feedstuffs. This caused Agriculture Minister James Ryan to propose, without success, that tobacco growing be reserved for smaller farmers (S11692); it was also the motivation behind the ill-conceived industrial alcohol scheme, which proposed using potatoes as a raw material. A possible reduction in oil imports was only a subordinate consideration. The idea, first mooted by the Commission on Industrial Resources (R10/7) and examined by a Senate commit-tee (Inds. Room 212/C15), did not receive serious consideration until 1932 when it was seen as offering a cash income to farmers who could not benefit from sugar beet or wheat. Lemass favored combin-ing a preliminary statement with the announcement of sugar factory locations to deflect the criticism of northern and western farmers.

Industry and Commerce proposed to establish a company that was controlled and financed by the state with a foreign technical and managerial team that would be paid a royalty. The proposal involved an investment of £1.5 million, the annual purchase of 400,000 tons of potatoes, and the employment of 750 workers. Petrol companies would be required to purchase and use a specified quantity of alcohol in a manner similar to wheat or tobacco, and this would lead to an increase in fuel prices. The resulting excise changes would entail an annual Exchequer loss of £330,000. Cabinet assent was granted in September 1933. When proposals for a company financed by the ICC did not materialize, Lemass decided to run the distilleries from his department, to the dismay of Finance who appear to have been excluded from the decision (Inds. Room 212/C44).

In an effort to spread the benefits it was decided to build five small distilleries. Fianna Fail cumainn [local chapters] in Butlersbridge and Dundalk wrote pressing their claims. Carrickmacross Urban District Council justified its entitlement on the grounds that it had "made a real effort for a beet factory" and that having recently completed a total of fifty-nine new houses, it was "absolutely necessary that the tenants, all of whom belong to the labouring classes, should be provided with the means whereby they could be able to pay their rents and thus avoid creating a burden on the rates" (Inds. Room 212 C/15). By early 1935 Leydon was considering plants at Ballina, Cooley, County Louth, two in Donegal, and a fifth in Carrickmacross or Donegal, though the Carrickmacross effluent would run into a lake where it would "make a stink." However, a deputation argued that it could be fed to pigs and or dumped in the river Glyde, so Carrickmacross won through.

The enterprise faced major difficulties; costs were substantially exceeded; production was delayed; all five plants were short of supplies. In the 1936–1937 season, Cooley, the sole plant in operation, had only six weeks' supplies. In the following season Cooley processed 7,000 tons and worked for 175 days; the other plants each processed 1,000 tons and worked for 25 days (S10392, TID 2/187). By 1940 all the plants processed 15,000–16,000 tons, 1% of potato output (CVO evid. 10657–663). Broken production runs led to cost increases. In 1937–1938 costs at Cooley, the most efficient plant, were estimated at almost 4s. per gallon, and the product was sold to petrol companies at 3*s.* per gallon, six times the cost of petrol. In 1938 Industry and Commerce was forced to recommend duty-free imports of molasses to provide adequate and cheaper raw material (Inds. Room 212/c43).

The industrial alcohol saga was the most ineffective self-sufficiency and decentralization operation undertaken, an unsavory example of Lemass's empire building and a classic illustration of the problem of investments absolved from conventional economic criteria. The decision to build five small distilleries increased costs; locations were determined by social and political factors. Ferguson justified the scheme as "a kind of social service for certain parts of the country"; however, two directors urged the establishment of an independent joint stock company subject "to the full rigours of government procedure" on the grounds that "as at present carried on it was liable to all sorts of political influence. From the point of view of purchase of raw materials, payment of wages etc. the obvious attitude of the farmers was to consider the Government 'fair game'" (Inds. R 212/c43). Direct administration by Industry and Commerce proved time consuming, as delegation appears to have been negligible, and it must have reduced effectiveness in other areas.[1] The most incisive criticism of the proposal was delivered before its establishment by John Leydon when he told Lemass that it would be better to "buy 400,000 tons of potatoes at 30/- per ton and distribute them among the poor and to employ 750 men the whole year round on, say, useful Public Health works at 30/- per week" with an annual saving of £444,000. Transfer payments such as unemployment assistance and infrastructural investment, which promoted employment in the building industry, were more beneficial to western areas (see table 7).

Decentralization overburdened an economy handicapped by lack of entrepreneurs, a dearth of managerial and technical skills, and restrictions on road transportation imposed to protect the railways (Skinner 1946, 65). The thin scattering of industrial plants reduced the gains from external economies and militated against the growth of an industrial culture—a deliberate government aim. Foreigners could be hired to meet shortages of key workers, though they suf-

---

1. This is the impression that emerges from Inds. R212/c19 and other related files.

TABLE 7

Employment in the Building Industry, 1926–1936

| Location | 1926 | | 1936 | | Gain | |
|---|---|---|---|---|---|---|
| | No. | % | No. | % | No. | % |
| Dublin City & Co. | 11,105 | 30.5 | 15,184 | 27.2 | 4,079 | 21.1 |
| Rest of Leinster | 7,602 | 20.9 | 13,210 | 23.7 | 5,608 | 29.0 |
| Munster | 13,194 | 36.2 | 17,323 | 31.1 | 4,129 | 21.3 |
| Connacht | 2,949 | 8.1 | 6,846 | 12.2 | 3,897 | 20.2 |
| Ulster | 1,606 | 4.4 | 3,201 | 5.7 | 4,129 | 8.2 |

*Source: Census of Population.*

fered from a restrictive licensing policy and from the xenophobic attitudes of the local work force who might protest at working under English supervision (Daly 1984b, 260–61).

For Fianna Fail these costs may have been offset by political dividends. The commitment to dispersal and evidence of scattered factories were undoubtedly popular, and the efforts of local committees were not unavailing. Father Hughes of Ballinasloe was rewarded with his factory (which still survives), and Carrickmacross was also successful. Criticism was directed at the inadequacy of decentralization rather than at its cost (Skinner 1946, 64). The procedure gave a populist veneer to a program charged with authoritarianism and provided opportunities for the exercise of political patronage thus ensuring Fianna Fail's long-term success.[2]

The Irish electorate has a long tradition of seeking political favors: nineteenth-century candidates were expected to deliver government patronage (Hoppen 1984, 74–83); by the end of the century the Congested Districts Board and Local Government Board opened up new sources of benevolence, and deputations pleading for new roads or famine relief were common. The Cosgrave administration introduced an unwelcome austerity in this regard. Much of the publicity given to the alleged famine of 1925 reflected disenchant-

2. For a more recent study of this process in operation see Paul Sacks, *The Donegal Mafia* (1976).

ment with its response. A Local Government inspector reporting on conditions on Achill Island at that time noted that "the appeals of the islanders and of those acting for them have perhaps been too generously met in the past and I am keenly alive to the spirit of depravity that exists among them and as a result of which they look outside the resources of the island for the wherewithal to live on. They look either to the harvests in England and Scotland or they seek Government aid. The existence of a native government alters the whole outlook" (S4278A). A Cumann na nGaedheal senator from Roscommon in 1926 charged that his constituents had been let down by the government in the matter of favors (Moss 1933, 105). Opportunities for favors were limited in the austere conditions of the twenties, but those that existed were not exercised. Olson has argued that large groups are less able to act in their common interest than are small groups; consequently the ability of individual towns to secure an industry at a cost to the wider community is not surprising. He also suggests that the benefits from redistribution outweigh the gains from economic growth (Olson 1976, 31). It was thus in the interests of Carrickmacross or Ballinasloe to secure a particular factory rather than to await the diluted benefits of economic growth.

Industrialists frequently used local groups to fight their case. The British shoe firm of Rawson opened a plant in Dundalk in response to a deputation and a promise of premises in the disused barracks (a favorite location). When its request for duty-free imports of shoe parts was rejected, the town clerk contacted local T.D. and Defense Minister Frank Aiken. The Dundalk Joint Representative Committee, which included the Urban District Council, the Chamber of Commerce, the Labour Council, and the Business Club, responded to an attack on Rawson's foreign status from the Irish Free State Boot Manufacturers Association with a resolution of support (TID 1207/7). Most deputations were led by a priest, reflecting bipartisan effort and continuing an earlier tradition. The involvement of politicians appears to have been only equal to that of business leaders.

*Capital and Labor: Corporatism*

The growth in government economic intervention in the interwar period and the apparent inappropriateness of legislatures as scrutinizing bodies led to the emergence in other parts of Europe of corporate institutions, which were perceived as better suited to contemporary needs. Although the 1922 Irish Constitution authorized the Oireachtas (Parliament) to provide for the establishment of Functional or Vocational Councils (J. Lee 1979, 325) and the Papal encyclical *Quadragesimo Anno* supported corporate structures, no such structures evolved. Under Cumann na nGaedheal institutional innovation tended towards centralization, as in the establishment of county and city managers. The state corporation, such as the Electricity Supply Board, was adopted for reasons of convenience rather than of principle and did not entail any wider corporate or consultative process. Cumann na nGaedheal's policies did not generate much need for new structures; Fianna Fail's program did.

In 1928 Lemass claimed that Fianna Fail "considered that the entire economic policy of the country should be decided by a National Economic Council such as exists in Germany and France and such as is suggested by one of the big English parties" (J. Lee 1979, 321); however, in 1932 De Valera admitted that although he had been in favor of establishing "something like an economic council," on gaining office he had rapidly discovered "that the Minister himself was carrying out the sort of survey that such an economic council would carry out" (PDDE 29 Apr. 1932). That corporatism had acquired fascist undertones and that Fine Gael had come to advocate corporatism (O'Sullivan 1940, 335) may have dictated inactivity. Centralized authority had also proved attractive, particularly to Lemass. Fianna Fail's public gestures were limited to instituting a corporate structure for the new Senate, and to establishing, on the proposal of opposition senators, a commission to inquire into the prospect of developing vocational organization in Ireland, though the commission's report had no practical consequences (J. Lee 1979, 324–46).

The Irish corporatist movement was weakened by lack of popular support. Catholic church support for corporatism had evolved in a situation where the church found itself in opposition to a state that upheld alien values (Berger 1972). In Ireland the state supported Catholic values. It is not surprising that corporatist ideas surfaced among groups such as cattle farmers who resented the disruption of their livelihood as a result of government action, but the battle against the state lacked broad support because the state reflected Irish and Catholic cultural values.

The failure to establish corporate institutions conceals the major changes undergone in government relations with business and labor and the existence of consultative structures. Throughout the 1920s, Industry and Commerce encouraged the establishment of industrial associations, maintaining regular contact and using them as sources for commercial intelligence; however, most sectors did not establish formal stuctures until after 1932. The delay is attributable to the lack of perceived benefits of association before that date. Cumann na nGaedheal was suspicious of interest groups, and the legislation establishing the Tariff Commission excluded industry groups. The Fianna Fail government brought a new receptiveness and much to lobby for. Where groups did not emerge spontaneously, officials willed them into existence. The Irish Wholesale Furniture Manufacturer's Association was formed in 1937 "in response to the Government's desire for a representative body to speak for the industry when tariff questions are being considered" (CVO pars. 231, 239, 276). When clothing manufacturers claimed prejudice against their goods from commercial travelers and drapers, Industry and Commerce suggested establishing a consultative committee of drapers, chambers of trade, and manufacturers (FII minutes 19 Oct. 1934), without success. Despite allegations to the contrary, there was frequent official contact with such bodies. During a debate on a furniture tariff Lemass told the Dail that he had met with the trade associations and regarded it as desirable to consult interested parties before imposing tariffs (PDDE 24 May 1932).

### Price Control

Most associations operated to ensure increased protection or higher prices. The tanning industry organized a successful campaign for specific minimum duties on leather despite Lemass's concern over the impact on the shoe industry (TID 23/73, box 255). Many associations exploited sympathy towards protection to raise prices. In 1938 a deputation from the structural steel industry was lectured about the "ultra high prices" that they charged, but they continued to seek higher tariffs and did little to cut prices (TID 41/27). Official control was hampered by the policy of granting tariffs without investigating costs and by Lemass's affinity for quotas and import licenses that excluded competing imports.

The 1932 Control of Prices Act provided for the establishment of a part-time Prices Commission and a full-time controller of prices with authority to control the price of food, drink, fuel, and clothing and the power to investigate the price of any protected item (PDDE 19 Oct. 1932). Many tariff schedules presented to the cabinet included price undertakings, as in the case of Irish Tapes, who sought a tariff increase from 50% to 100% but undertook not to increase prices. The agreement with Irish Dunlop included an undertaking that the retail price for tires would not exceed British prices by more than 15%; however, the undertaking lapsed in the event of any change in relative costs between Dunlop's British and Irish plants (S6560A). Requests for extraordinarily high levels of duty, ostensibly to prevent dumping, coupled with undertakings of limited or no price increase were common, but it is unclear whether they were fulfilled. In 1937, in the course of amending legislation, Lemass told the Dail that the Prices Commission had investigated the price of wheaten meal, bread, heavy fuel oil, building materials, furniture, and mattresses.

The 1937 Act substituted three full-time price commissioners, substantially extended their investigative powers, and empowered them to fix prices and to report on causes of "unreasonable" prices (PDDE 6 Oct. 1937), but there is no evidence that the increased powers were used. While there is evidence of official concern about some prices, pressure appears to have been exercised through informal channels and was directed at the prices of intermediate goods. The Ever-Ready Battery Company was forced to reduce prices, though this failed to stem imports (TID 1207/166). In 1938 Lemass ordered an investigation of leather prices. It is no coincidence that batteries and leather were intermediate products. One official minuted, "If leather was a commodity going direct to the consumer one would have less hesitation in recommending a high rate of protection. But when a very important industry is affected I submit that a very strong case should be made before increased duties are imposed" (TID 43/63, box 255). There is no evidence that lower prices were enforced by reducing protection, though Lemass threatened such steps against a doll factory if the quality did not improve (PDDE 27 Oct. 1937).

The increased costs resulting from protection have been estimated at £9 million in 1936, a rise of 27% over the free market level,
though tariffs averaged 45%; the increase on nonfood items was
considerably higher (Ryan 1949, 302). These figures may overstate
the inflationary impact. The Irish Cost of Living Index stood at 177
in November 1937, against 160 for Britain and Northern Ireland;
for January 1926, the figures were 188 and 175. Prior to 1932, a
12-13-point gap appears to be the norm, compared with 17 points in
1937 (*ITJ* December 1937).

Lax control over prices and profits appears to have been the
inevitable consequence of rapid industrial development, as a memorandum by T. G. Smiddy, De Valera's economic advisor, on the 1937
prices bill shows. Smiddy claimed that if the Prices Commission
used all the powers available under the bill it would replicate the
investigation carried out by the Tariff Commission before 1932,
though he argued that the prices commission should be independent
of Industry and Commerce (S9490). Yet in 1932 Lemass had admitted that detailed price investigation would spell an end to industrial
development. "If we are going to let the factor of prices determine
our position as to whether or not an industry is to be established here,
then we can abandon the whole idea of industrial development at
once. There is no single industrial commodity which we are capable
of producing here which we could not buy more cheaply somewhere
[else]" (PDDE 13 May 1932).

There is no accurate information on the extent of private fortunes resulting from protection, but accusations that Fianna Fail
policies had resulted, perhaps "unintentionally" in the creation of "a
kind of new plutocracy of economic privilege" (PDSE 14 Dec. 1938)
among those with access to licenses or monopolies were frequent
though unsustained. Some fortunes were accumulated, though fewer
than critics might suggest, because industrialists faced a powerful
trade union movement and were forced to meet a variety of social
criteria.

### Trade Union Membership

Trade union membership and bargaining power increased as a
result of protection. Membership had grown rapidly during the war

and in the years immediately following but fell in the early twenties, a pattern common to other European countries. Returns to the Registrar of Friendly Societies show a decline from almost 140,000 members in 1921 to less than 89,000 by 1927 and to 86,000 by 1931. By 1939 numbers had risen to 135,000. The 1937 annual report of the largest union, the Irish Transport and General Workers Union (ITGWU), recorded the seventh consecutive year of growth; the British-based, National Union of Boot and Shoe Operatives (NUBSO) saw its Irish membership grow from 378 in 1932 to 4,224 by 1937 (Fox, 1958, 528); membership of the Irish Women Workers Union doubled between 1925 and 1938 (CVO, 185).

Industrial employment grew without a drop in real wages, one index of trade union effectiveness. Real wages of adult male workers in Dublin were 10% higher in 1936 than in 1929, which was identical to the rise in United Kingdom real wages; by 1934, Dublin laborers, who traditionally earned less than their London equivalents, were apparently earning more. The Banking Commission concluded that "from 1929 to 1936 wages rates were maintained better in Dublin than in London" (CBC 1938, 63), and trends in the regions were not dissimilar as union organizers sought, contrary to government wishes, to maintain uniform wage levels throughout the country (McCarthy 1977, 182).

In industries such as boots and shoes, flour milling, hosiery and textiles, joint industrial councils or conciliation boards representing employers and workers negotiated wage levels, frequently with government participation (CVO, 199–202). Both workers and employers were aware that protection cushioned them against competition. Mr. Cunningham of the Boot and Shoe Manufacturers Association claimed that "the Union" (NUBSO) asked for higher wages "because the industry is so well protected here"; it was "only after considerable discussion that we were able to get the existing Irish rates down to the English rate" (Curtis 1981, 34). British unions ensured that Irish wages and working conditions would prevent Irish plants' competing in British or third-country markets. Lionel Poole, Irish national organizer for NUBSO told his members in 1933 that "we cannot prevent our industry from spreading itself into districts that it has not been established in previously but we can prevent this position from becoming a danger to other centres. This is our task in the Free State" (Fox 1958, 482).

The union position was strengthened by a superficial identity between unions' social aims and those of the government. While the revised constitution of the Irish Trades Union Congress in 1930 retained a commitment to securing "adequate control of the industries and services" for all workers, more radical wording was rejected, and this commitment did not interfere with more prosaic goals. In her presidential address to the 1932 conference, Louie Bennett praised the new government, "which has brought a wave of hope and vitality into depressed and apathetic ranks" (McCarthy 1977, 97, 112). The 1932 annual report of the ITGWU expressed its support for protection and for the policy of industrial dispersal, criticizing only the excessive employment of women and juveniles and poor working conditions (ITGWU Annual Report 1932). The government proved receptive to suggested reforms in these areas because of sensitivity to opposition gibes that Irish industry was "a hole and corner development" and because of its aim to expand industry "without the evils of industrialisation as they have manifested themselves in other countries" (*IT* 24 Jan. 1934).

### Conditions of Employment Act

Such considerations resulted in the 1936 Conditions of Employment Act, which created "an industrial code far ahead of that in force in any other country" (*Economist,* 2 Jan. 1937). Lemass boasted that "so far as I know" it was the first time that such measures had been introduced by "a Government that is still a democratic Government dependent entirely upon a Parliamentary institution for its power" (PDDE 17 May 1935). The act was influenced by International Labour Organisation decrees, and its passage was duly rewarded by Lemass becoming ILO president in 1937 (Skinner 1946, 66). The adult working week was set at forty-eight hours, and the working day was to end at eight PM, with limited exemptions; overtime was restricted and was to be paid in excess of normal rates. Shift work was forbidden except for continuous process operations or when licensed, and employers were required to document piecework rates. Workers were guaranteed one week's holiday with pay in addition to six public holidays and were protected against wage reductions consequent on reduced working hours. Wage agreements between a representative group of employers and workers could be registered and made legally enforceable. Employment of persons under fourteen was forbidden; those under eighteen were restricted to a forty-hour week and could be restricted or banned from an industry following consultation with employer and worker representatives. The minister could restrict the employment of women in a similar manner, and both women and young people were barred from night work, though limited exemptions were possible for young people. A ban on outworking, or manufacture in homes, could be imposed by ministerial order (*ITJ* June 1936).

Lemass informed the cabinet that "if employment is to be balanced in the Saorstat, certain avenues must be reserved for men." Women accounted for 75% to 90% of workers in industries such as clothing, packing, shoes, and confectionery, and unlike other countries, Ireland did not have substantial male employment in heavy industries. At one stage Lemass apparently toyed with banning the use of modern machinery on the grounds that it facilitated the employment of women, but he opted for statutory restriction, arguing that "without it, women may rapidly be recruited for most classes of industry that are likely to be developed here."

Lemass's proposals were supported by cabinet colleagues, and Finance raised few objections. The costs of reducing working hours without wage reduction were not examined; Leydon merely noted that "the additional expenditure entailed by such a proposal will be borne by the employer" (S84/14/35). In the Dail, opposition speakers united in welcoming the bill. Criticism, which was muted, consisted of Labour suggestions that more could be done and of familiar comments on the excessive ministerial powers, though there were differences of opinion on the merits of nominating public holidays rather than church holidays as designated days off work. Sean Milroy, president of the Federation of Irish Industries, welcomed the control on "back-room factories" and the prospect of policing firms that undercut responsible employers (*IT* 9 May 1935), while Sen. James G. Douglas, a speaker for manufacturing interests, approved the general principles, though he noted the act's cost implications (PDSE 27 Nov. 1935). This public stance appears to reflect the attitude of the Federation of Irish Industries (FII). In 1933 the committee of the

FII voted to support a 40-hour week (FII minutes 2 June 1933); in the Dail Lemass mentioned that employers who had made generous agreements with workers often requested that the terms be enforced on competitors.

The acquiesence to the terms of the Conditions of Employment Act at a time when Irish political life was deeply riven over nationalist matters reflects a broad consensus for an economic middle ground among employers, workers, and politicians. Several politicians mentioned the absence of an "anti-Labour" movement in Ireland. Both employers and unions sought protection from cost undercutting in the domestic market. Trade union opinion viewed the reduction of working hours and the curbs on female and juvenile employment as essential to reduce unemployment.

Union support was universal save for the Irish Women Workers Union, which objected to restrictions on female employment, a cause that elicited little support as the ITUC had submitted a memorandum to Lemass favoring restrictions (M. Jones 1988, 130). Senator Thomas Foran, president of the ITGWU, which had approximately 6,000 female members (Daly 1978, 73), denounced the opposition of women trade unionists: "Do the feminists want here what occurs in certain industrial countries across the water where the men mind the babies and the women go to the factories? Do they want that in this holy Ireland of ours" (PDSE 27 Nov. 1935). Yet even women trade unionists were ambivalent on this question, as they were in other countries. In a speech, Louie Bennett, president of the IWWU in 1932, concluded that the increasing employment of women in industry had been detrimental to family life and a possible cause of male unemployment and consequently of increased poverty. In 1942 Mrs. Margaret Purtell of the Tailors and Garment Workers Union requested a ministerial order barring women from much of the tailoring trade (Daly 1978, 75, 77). Popular attitudes favored male jobs, as a deputation from Mountmellick revealed. One hapless official noted, "The deputation was not in the least impressed. Fr. Murray said they wanted to find employment for men, Bat Leather Co. was employing girls" (TID 43/75).

The perception of juvenile and female encroachment into the industrial work force was correct, though overall female employment showed only a minor increase: gains in industry were offset by losses in agriculture and domestic service. In 1936 women accounted for

TABLE 8

Employment by Sex, 1926 and 1936

| Item | Male | | | Female | | |
|------|------|------|------|--------|------|------|
| | 1926 | 1936 | Gain | 1926 | 1936 | Gain |
| *C. Pop.* trans. gds. | 86,742 | 94,594 | 8,152 | 31,477 | 43,215 | 11,738 |
| *C. Prod.* trans. gds. | 41,112 | 64,045 | 22,933 | 17,358 | 37,271 | 19,913 |

31.3% of the manufacturing work force compared with 26.6% ten years earlier. According to the production census the number of workers under eighteen more than doubled, from 6,619 in 1926 to 16,355 in 1936: 5.9% of male and 24% of female workers (see table 8). The increased juvenile and female employment, which was in line with international developments, was a result of the expansion of light industries rather than of a substitution of female for male workers. The female and juvenile share of the Irish work force remained below U.K. levels (*C. prod.* 1936, xvi, xxi). During the decade 1936–1946 women and juveniles declined as a proportion of the industrial work force. Although women accounted for an increasing proportion of workers in clothing, textiles, and boots and shoes, the expansion of heavy industry meant more male jobs (see table 9). The 1936 production census anticipated a falling proportion of juvenile workers as apprentices recruited by new industries reached the age of eighteen.

No formal restrictions were imposed on juvenile or female workers as a result of the Conditions of Employment Act, though there was an undoubted preference for male jobs. An official who visited two British tanneries to negotiate an Irish operation reported with enthusiasm that Dickens tanners had "no women employed and even the typing is done by male labour" (TID 43/63); this may have led to Dickens's being favored over another firm. When Ever-Ready expressed an interest in an Irish plant Lemass minuted that "my raising no objection to this project depends on their employing men and I am prepared to contemplate prices higher than in Great Britain if necessary because of this." Some years later the company successfully justified a claim for increased protection on the grounds of their maximum male employment (TID 1207/166).

TABLE 9

Women and Juveniles in the Industrial Work Force
*(in percentage)*

| | Female | | | |
| | (% all pop.) | | Juvenile M | Juvenile F |
| Year | Industry | Trans. Gds. | (% M pop.) | (% F pop.) |
|------|----------|-------------|------------|------------|
| 1926 | 18.8 | 29.7 | 3.6 | 17.8 |
| 1936 | 24.7 | 36.4 | 5.9 | 24.0 |
| 1938 | 24.1 | 37.4 | 5.8 | 18.2 |
| 1943 | 25.6 | 36.3 | 5.8 | 15.6 |

Lemass claimed that the purpose of the legislation was "not to secure employment for men now unemployed but to arrest any tendency to increasing female for male labour" (PDDE 17 May 1935). However, the existence of powers to curb female employment may have exerted psychological pressure on employers. In 1937 the male share of the adult work force rose; men gained relative to women, adults relative to juveniles. An official noted, "So long as adult labour stands at 80% and upwards and so long as the figure for men does not decrease in favour of that for women, the type of labour provided in the protected industries cannot be regarded as undesirable" (F200/27/ 38).

The Conditions of Employment Act appears to have brought escalating wages without industrial peace. The year 1937 was marked by a lengthy building dispute and by rising wage rates as a result of inflation. The FIM argued in evidence to the Commission on Vocational Organisation that the legislation "while in itself desirable has been advanced too rapidly in favour of the industrial worker," citing the fact that in 10 out of 13 industries Irish wages exceeded British levels (CVO evid. FIM memo, 5). Industrialists used alleged cost increases consequent on the legislation as justification for further protection (TID 21/43). By 1941 only 1 of more than 180 agreements had been registered under the act, and the government had rejected several agreements that enforced a uniform national rate of pay (McCarthy 1977,183).

## *Relations with Employers and Unions*

Concessions on price, wages, and protective legislation should not be read as a sign of government weakness. Control remained in government hands, and because of such concessions, industry and the unions were expected to facilitate the government's industrial design. Relations proved stormy with both on occasion as they opposed what they regarded as authoritarianism. The key issue revolved around native control. Both employers and trade unionists were affected by the heady nationalism of Irish independence, which was boosted after 1932 by the Fianna Fail government and the economic war. Traditional employer interests were unionist, and during the twenties the Dublin Chamber of Commerce and the Association of Chambers of Commerce adopted a conservative business stance, fearful of government intervention and committed to retaining economic links with Britain. They were opposed to the economic war— not surprising given the dominance of shipping, importing, and commercial interests (Cullen 1983, 95–105). Nationalist-minded businessowners were concentrated in the DIDA and its successor the NAIDA. Efforts to turn the NAIDA into a manufacturers' interest group by insisting that the chair be a manufacturer were foiled in 1930 (NAIDA minutes 2 June 1930), and Irish manufacturers had no representative organization prior to 1932, though a short-lived Federation of Irish Industries existed for part of the twenties.

A new Federation of Irish Industries was founded in December 1932. The foreword to its minutes stated that as a result of the election of a government committed to protection it was felt desirable to have an organization dealing exclusively with manufacturers' interests. Membership was restricted to Irish nationals so that "Irishmen alone will have the government, ruling and guiding of the Federation in its work for the welfare and development of home industry" (*Ir. Ind. Yrbook.* 1932), and this remained the tone of the organization. It sought improved access to finance, differential tax treatment for capital invested in Irish-owned industries, and insuring "as far as possible consistent with national requirements (that) industrial development shall be retained in the hands of Saorstat nationals" (FII minutes, foreword).

Despite common aims relations with the government were strained. In its submission to the Commission on Vocational Organization the federation complained of a lack of consultation on industrial planning and specifically of a failure to ask FII whether there was room for new factories "in industrial fields already provided for." This statement is misleading. An Industry and Commerce official attended FII Council meetings and acted as liaison officer, and Lemass used Federation events to air his plans for the development of industry. More detailed blueprints were raised informally by Lemass or officials in regular meetings with individual industrial groups. Consultation was frequent, though on the government's terms, and the federation's views had no formal status. The key issue was the government's denying the FII a veto over the course of industrial development and particularly over the admission of foreign firms. The Control of Manufactures Act gave some native industrialists the mistaken belief that irrespective of competence, they were guaranteed a monopoly.

While the federation's lobbying was one factor in the 1934 strengthening of the Control of Manufactures Act, the legislation fell short of their wishes. When Lemass was seen to welcome foreign firms, FII's bitterness was evident. Former Cumann na nGaedheal minister and federation activist J. J. Walsh wrote:

> Is it any wonder therefore, that great numbers of nationalists are disillusioned at the turn of events. Their long and bitter fight was waged for economic as well as cultural regeneration. They had hoped that a Government of their own would see to it that, whatever eventuated from the former, would pass to them as their natural right. Instead, not only did the enemy of their country get almost everything worth taking but the native taxpayer was compelled in many cases to supply him with the necessary finance to do so, through the Industrial Credit Company. (Walsh 1944, 88–89)

The issue of foreign companies came to a head over the proposal to establish the Salts spinning mill, which aroused considerable opposition because wool spinning was viewed as a traditional Irish industry. Allegations that Industry and Commerce had rejected proposals for a spinning mill from the Cork firm of Sunbeam Wolsey (which had 49% foreign ownership) were widely aired in newspapers and in the Dail prior to the 1937 general election; however, closer examination by the council of the FII revealed that the Sunbeam Wolsey proposal "could not be turned down when they had not put up a scheme to the Department." Lemass claimed that his officials had repeatedly urged the Woollen Manufacturers Association to set up a spinning operation but that "they were not prepared to cooperate with the Department even though inducements in the way of Trade Loans were offered to them." While individual manufacturers suffered selective amnesia the FII's investigation confirmed Lemass's version of events (FII minutes 1937).

Despite this finding, the federation passed a resolution that FII should explore the possibility of establishing any industry with 100% Irish capital and control before government assistance was given to firms not wholly controlled by Irish nationals. A decision to publish the resolution brought a split between moderates such as Sen. James G. Douglas, who favored "a line of friendly co-operation," and the militant majority led by F. M. Summerfield, F. H. O'Donnell, and J. J. Walsh (FII minutes 15 Oct. 1937). Walsh's membership on the Commission on Vocational Organisation explains why "the Report singled out the Department of Industry and Commerce for particular criticism" (J. Lee 1979, 331).

The FII demand for control of new industrial investment is reminiscent of the powers that Mussolini ceded to the Italian industrial confederation to evaluate license applications for new industrial plants. Italian industrialists used this power to increase their monopoly: of more than 5,000 licenses to set up industry issued in the years 1933–1940 only 414 had been instituted by 1945 (Sarti 1971, 108–9). Irish industrial interests are unlikely to have acted in a more disinterested manner. The continued obsession of the FII with native control and its unwillingness to admit "alien" industrialists weakened its claim to a consultative role. In Feb. 1938 FII changed its name to the Federation of Irish Manufacturers to mark amalgamation with the NAIDA; however, the new constitution emphasized that individual members must be Irish citizens, while corporate

membership was restricted to firms where "legal and financial control of the business is bona fide in the hands of persons who are
citizens of Ireland" (FIM minutes 18 Feb. 1938).

FIM protested strongly against the government's failure to
consult the federation prior to the 1938 Anglo-Irish Trade Agreement, because British manufacturers had allegedly been consulted by
the British Board of Trade. The 1938 agreement forced a reconsidera-
tion of the federation's role. As federation president F. M. Summerfield
pointed out, the federation had been "living in a fool's paradise for
the last few years." The agreement provided for the strengthening of
the Irish Prices Commission to review tariff levels; however, interests
applying to the commission would have to represent both native and
foreign firms.

By 1939 the individual industry associations had admitted
foreign firms, but the federation proved reluctant to follow suit. F. M.
Summerfield pointed out "that a great number of industries which it
was alleged were non-national had, in fact become permanent institutions in the country, who are very much concerned to preserve their
position, and that no Government at the present time or in the next
few years was likely to turn them out" (FIM minutes 6 Jan. 1939).
Ultimately many new firms were admitted to the federation, and
total membership rose by 130 to 600 by the end of 1939, though this
was allegedly done "without altering essentially the general beliefs of
the members of the Council regarding the national position" (FIM
minutes 1938–1940).

The more pragmatic approach appears to be linked with the
appointment of Erskine Childers, formerly secretary of NAIDA, as
federation secretary in 1938. Childers was also Fianna Fail T.D. for
Longford Westmeath, combining both positions until 1944 when he
became a minister (Skinner 1946, 302). The contrast in styles is
evident in the Commission on Vocational Organization where Walsh
excoriates the government for lack of consultation and "alien penetration" while the federation's official memorandum concentrated
on labor productivity and problems of industrial relations.

"Alien penetration" was also an issue in the Irish trade union
movement, though in this case Lemass showed greater sympathy for
native concern. The issue was compounded by the mass of unions in
each industry representing different crafts and by the rivalry between

British and Irish unions. Interunion disputes seem to have intensified after 1932 and the substantial recruitment by British-based unions was a further cause of friction. The 1935 report of the ITUC wrote of "warring competitive unions, disintegrating new bodies and internecine union warfare" (McCarthy 1977, 134). In 1934 the ITUC invited all foreign-based unions to attend a conference to examine the question of their Irish membership. Congress president Tom Johnson (who was English-born) stated that the national executive "merely asked the amalgamated unions to do for this country, long before any crisis arose, what was found to be needed in other countries. . . . There was growing up a different code of laws, a different legislative atmosphere affecting Trade Unions in this country from that which prevailed in Britain." However the meeting resulted in the creation of a united block of British-based unions within the ITUC (McCarthy 1977, 124, 126) determined to remain in Ireland.

Following this lack of progress Lemass informed Congress in 1936 that if it did not rationalize the trade unions, the state would intervene. Congress appointed a commission of enquiry, which issued a report in 1939, sharply divided between those favoring little change and ITGWU proposals to reduce the British trade union presence and to increase ITGWU influence. This split led to the 1941 trade union bill, which drew heavily on the ITGWU proposals. All unions were to be licensed and forced to maintain offices and money within the state—measures designed to discourage British unions—and a tribunal would rationalize the trade union structure. While the measure became law it failed in its intent. British unions survived, and rationalization was thwarted.

## Conclusion

Irrespective of the government's wishes, because of divisions within manufacturer and union ranks strong corporate structures would not have emerged. Evidence from continental countries suggests that the growth of democratic corporatism was the product of a long historical tradition. Ireland lacked that tradition and faced the problem that the Irish business elite—based on export-oriented

agriculture and industry and on close Anglo-Irish commercial links—
was in the throes of disruption, while a new protectionist business
community was emerging. The trade union movement was equally
in flux. The largest union, the ITGWU, was less than thirty years
old. Both business and labor required a lengthy maturing period.

While both groups benefited from protection they failed to
shift their concern from sectional interests to a wider national agenda.
Government carrots such as high tariffs, lack of price controls or the
Conditions of Employment Act do not appear to have elicited recip-
rocal concessions; the extensive protection afforded to both unions
and employers only led to entrenched positions.

Ultimately the responsibility may lie with the government,
which communicated the message of protection and native control
only too effectively while ignoring issues of efficiency and productivity. Legislative curbs on female employment and decentralization of
industry signaled that Ireland was elevating social desiderata above
economic criteria and provided justification for employer and labor
entrenchment.

The report of the FII to the Commission on Vocational
Organisation, though partisan in that it ignores manufacturers' weaknesses, highlights the low productivity in Irish industry. The problem was seen as stemming from a lack of industrial tradition,
compounded by the shift to cattle farming, by population decline,
and by emigration, all serving to "creat(e) an atmosphere not conducive to the necessity for work for the sake of high production through
the necessity of earning as high a wage as is possible where work is
paid for by results." Case histories cited included a firm in a village
employing small farmers' sons who regularly disappeared for two
days at a time, arriving late on Monday mornings and going absent
for race meetings; and a Donegal factory where workers did not
desire to earn more than a minimum weekly amount and consequently kept output low, where absenteeism on Monday mornings or
on wet days, despite facilities for drying and changing clothes, was
common. In one area devoid of industrial traditions girls recorded
productivity levels 32% below what they had achieved during their
overseas training (CVO evid. doc. 92). It seems probable that employers also took time off for race meetings and had "unambitious
and unproductive" natures, though this was never stated. More

common were criticisms of a "new plutocracy." Both statements suggest that Irish society had not adopted the cultural values of a modern industrial society.

The most sustained attack on the government's economic program came from the report of the Banking Commission. The report decided that the existing banking system and the link with sterling should be retained but feared that prevailing policies could jeopardize the sterling link by reducing the country's external investments and by weakening export earnings. It rejected the possibility that new industries could contribute to export earnings: their prices were uncompetitive and would remain so because government economic regulation had given rise to "an element of rigidity" in the economy (CBC 1938, 132, 106, 181). The prescription was a curb on government borrowing and no further self-sufficiency lest it further damage export earnings.

Such comments emphasised the need to control the excesses of the protected economy. While De Valera countered criticism of the "new plutocracy" by arguing his commitment to private property and to the right of an individual to earn a "reasonable profit," some of the alleged gains from the industrial program accorded ill with his description of the policies as providing "the material necessities of life" and "amenities which are necessary for decent living," and he admitted that policies had failed to absorb the unemployed (PDDE 7 July 1935). Given the criticism expressed by the Banking Commission, the apparent failure of programs such as decentralization, and the perceived ingratitude of both manufacturers and trade unions despite numerous benefits, it would seem that threat of competition and the questioning of the industrialization program resulting from the 1938 Anglo-Irish agreement were not wholly unwelcome.

# 7 The Financial Sector
## Continuity and Change

THE FIANNA FAIL blueprint required increased capital resources and new institutions to handle them. In 1929 Lemass had expressed determination to reduce the extent of foreign investment by the banking and insurance sectors (Gallagher Papers MS 18339) by developing an Irish financial center and money market (CBC 1938, evid 395). This plan posed a major threat to established financial institutions that increased with the founding of the state industrial bank, the Industrial Credit Company. However, Fianna Fail never attempted a radical break in financial policy, and although Lemass proposed the establishment of a state bank to fund public works and a break with sterling in November 1932 (S6222), there is no evidence that such steps were considered.[1]

The years following 1932 brought changes in the structure of Irish capital holdings, a state industrial credit company, and increased taxes on banking, but in contrast to the attempted revolutions in industry and agriculture, the Irish pound retained parity with sterling and 100% sterling backing, while Irish commercial banks retained close links with the London financial market. At a time when sterling's international role had weakened, and deferential dominions such as Australia and South Africa broke with sterling

1. Unless otherwise stated, figures in this chapter come from *Statistical Abstracts* for various years in the 1930s and from annual reports of the *Companies Office*; share values and dividends come from the Stock Exchange share listings.

and established central banks, Ireland retained the sterling links. There was logic to this continuity. Sterling was no longer over valued following the 1931 decision to leave the gold standard. Continuity in financial policy reflected the lack of a developed money market and continuing links with the British economy. In 1934 economist Henry Clay noted that a country without a money market must link itself with one of the larger financial markets and that Ireland, like Denmark, would naturally link with Britain because of the volume of mutual trade (BI, secretary's file).

By 1932, the banking community, which had displayed open hostility to the new state, had achieved a certain coexistence that survived the election of Fianna Fail. The 1929 Bank of Ireland Act had required a majority of shareholders in the state's largest financial institution to be natives of the Saorstat, and this may have preempted more radical intervention under Fianna Fail, while the appointment of Lord Glenavy, the former Gordon Campbell, as governor of the Bank of Ireland and the decision in 1932 to finance trade loans following years of refusal (Daly 1984a) signified a new accommodation.

A commission of inquiry into banking, currency, and credit, appointed by the minister for finance in November 1934, provided further reassurance. Its majority report, published in 1938, concluded that the system was "a well-designed and well-built, well-driven piece of mechanism, in first class working order and condition" (CBC 1938, pars. 5–12). It recommended the establishment of a central bank, financed and largely controlled by the commercial banks. The conservative tone of the report reflects the commission's membership, which was dominated by Irish and foreign bankers and by the Department of Finance, with Joseph Brennan, former secretary of finance, as chairman. Although the commission heard numerous witnesses, it received no formal testimony from either the Department of Finance or from the Irish banks, an omission that may reflect the belief that such testimony would prove superfluous in the light of their almost total control over proceedings. Virtually all criticism was directed at government policy and at aspects that might result in departures from the banking status quo.

In the absence of formal testimony from the banks, it is difficult to pinpoint their precise views on Fianna Fail policy. The best guide is probably provided by the memorandum contributed by Lord Glenavy, a member of the commission, who signed the majority report but appended a twenty-one-page memorandum (CBC 1938, add. 2) that trumpeted the commission's satisfaction with the Irish banking system. He emphasized its dependence on "two buttresses," overseas investments and bank deposits, and attacked policies that might injure either factor, such as the establishment of the Agricultural Credit Company which competed on unequal terms for deposits, or efforts to encourage domestic investment at the expense of foreign holdings.

Bank deposits fell by over £12 million in the years 1931–1935 (CBC 1938, par. 123), reflecting the impact of recession on the farming community, which accounted for 39% of deposits in 1937 (CBC 1938, add. 2, par. 20), and the attraction of new investments. Bank of Ireland dividends fell from 17.5% from 1926 to 1931 and 13.5% from 1932 to 1939 (Hall 1946, app. H).

*External Investments and New Company Formation*

Irish external investments declined during the 'thirties, though not at a rate to occasion concern. No balance of payments figures exist before 1933 and the early figures give rise to suspicion as certain sums tend to recur year after year (For example, £550,000 was recorded each year from 1933 to 1936 as representing the net outflow of insurance company investments.). In 1932 Irish external investments were estimated at £170 million, £70 million invested in gilts (£50 million of this held by Irish banks) and £100 million in industrial securities (11 May 1932); by 1936 external investments had fallen by £10 million (CBC 1938 evid. par. 2921). British economist Geoffrey Crowther, in a memorandum on credit policy prepared for the Bank of Ireland in October 1932, noted that the external assets of the Irish banks exceeded liabilities by £83.5 million, a sum that "probably represents a higher proportionate amount of foreign assets than is possessed by any other banking system of the world" (Bank of Ireland, credit policy memo., 4).

The 1930s were characterized by a reorientation in investment patterns and by substantial capital inflow. In 1932, the first year for which figures are available, 31.2% of commercial banking assets were invested in the Free State compared with 37.5% in 1939, an increase concentrated in the private sector. The shift indicates responsiveness to an increased demand for capital and a more profitable domestic environment. Bankers and historians (Olleranshaw 1988, 222–32) have argued that the level of external investments reflected the lack of profitable domestic opportunities. This shift may have averted pressure for government action. By 1936 Leydon believed that there was no evidence of a shortage of business capital (CBC 1938, par. 1817).

*Insurance*

While the banks escaped largely unscathed the insurance industry was subjected to significant intervention. By the late 1920s approximately 80% of insurance business was under British control; the majority of native firms were insolvent, and the industry invested the overwhelming majority of its premiums outside Ireland, an annual capital drain of £1 million. Insurance companies had invested a mere £90,000 in Irish government securities; unlike their British counterparts they did not finance government-guaranteed loans, and they held negligible investments in Irish industrial securities. Cumann na nGaedheal set up a commission of inquiry into the insurance industry in 1926 that produced no concrete results, probably because the report revealed major ideological differences between the majority, including John Leydon, then of Finance, which refused to regard external investment as a drain on resources and dismissed allegations of a shortage of capital, and the minority, including J. Barrington of Industry and Commerce who urged state control to redress the inevitability of foreign control and to channel capital into the Irish economy (S2348, S4989).

The draft legislation adopted in 1934 provided for the amalgamation of weak companies, under compulsion if necessary, and the creation, with state assistance, of one or more Irish firms; only Irish-registered companies with at least 60% native shareholding would be permitted to engage in nonlife insurance; all companies would be obliged to invest in the domestic market; and a state reinsurance company would be established. The process of amalgamation proved

TABLE 10

Annual Averages of Securities Holdings
in Estates Subject to Death Duties
*(in pounds sterling)*

| Group | 1926–1930 | 1934–1938 |
|---|---|---|
| Brit. and for. govts. | 1,948,803 | 1,958,839 |
| Brit. and for. co. shares | 3,263,440 | 3,284,723 |
| Irish govt. and mun. | 312,907 | 1,042,721 |
| Irish co. shares | 1,394,149 | 1,824,623 |

*Source:* Statistical Abstracts.

more time-consuming than was anticipated. Several English companies sold their Irish holdings, and the vested interests of small Irish
companies proved difficult to appease. Ultimately the Irish Life
Insurance Company was created, with the government as majority
shareholder. While the requirement to invest in the Irish market was
not enforced, the strengthening of the native insurance industry and
the emergence of a state-owned company increased the proportion
domestically invested, though the failure to establish an Irish
reinsurance company ensured a continuing outflow (S2349, S9441A).

*Irish Investment Holdings*

The register of British government and India stocks held at the
Bank of Ireland by Saorstat residents declined from £97 million in
1923 to £72.8 million by 1929 and £52.5 million by 1940, though
this trend reflects the emigration or death of stockholders rather than
the transfer of investments. Irish estate duty statistics suggest no
decline in foreign investment holdings among those dying in Ireland
in 1926–1930 and 1934–1938 though there was a substantial increase in holdings of Irish securities (see table 10). The growth of
Irish holdings reflects an increase in the number and value of Irish
enterprises. Companies Office records show a rise in the number of
registered companies from 1,803 in 1931 to 2,832 by 1939. The

number of companies registered averaged 120 in the years 1925–
1931 and 209 for 1932–1939. The paid-up value of registered
companies rose from £36 million in 1925 to £37.9 million by
December 1931 and £50.8 million by the end of 1939. The average
annual value of new companies was £3.98 million for the years
1932–1939 more than treble 1925–1931 values. Companies registered in 1931 were valued at £670,200 compared with £1.7 million
in 1932 and £8.4 million in 1933. By 1939 there was a total of 360
public companies with a paid-up capital of £27.4 million and 2,472
private companies with a paid-up capital of £23.4 million. The
majority had a nominal share capital of less than £10,000.

*The Stock Exchange*

The total value of shares quoted on the Dublin Stock Exchange
in 1933 amounted to £3.25 million, and new issues in the preceding
three years had been a mere £160,750 (Industrial Credit Co. annual
report 1936). In 1934 new industrial issues valued at £2.8 million
were launched and new industrial issues in the period 1933–1939
totalled over £7.9 million (Industrial Credit Co. AGM Dec. 1934,
Dec. 1939). The flurry of business was a consequence of protection
and the desire to fulfill share-holding requirements under the Control of Manufactures Acts. The 1932 Finance Act provided an income tax concession of 20% on investments in Irish public companies,
though Dublin stockbrokers were divided as to the significance of
this measure (CBC 1938, evid. 2926). The greatest incentive was
probably the buoyant share market. The Dublin market had fallen
steadily throughout the years 1922–1926, in contrast to London,
though it recovered somewhat in the years 1927–1929, and the 1929
fall was significantly less than in London. The years 1931–1938 saw
a sustained rise that outstripped the London market (Thomas 1986,
182).

The source of these funds remains a matter of dispute. One
witness on behalf of the stock exchange told the Banking Commission that every industrial issue was accompanied by a sale of foreign
securities (CBC 1938 evid, pars. 2879–2905) and claimed that over
the preceding two years, sales of securities other than government

securities practically balanced purchases of Saorstat securities. This impression is not backed by statistics. Figures on stock exchange transactions carried out by Saorstat brokers suggest that purchases and sales of foreign securities were virtually in balance over the years 1933–1939, while figures for net investment income from abroad show no obvious decline. Official figures record a net capital inflow of £10.4 million in 1933 and £7.5 million in 1934, small net outflows in 1935 and 1936, and inflows of over £5 million in both 1937 and 1938. Part of this inflow was a result of the fall in Irish external assets, but £12 million is unaccounted for, suggesting substantial investment in Ireland by foreigners during the thirties (or inaccuracies in balance of payment statistics). Officials estimated that foreign-held capital accounted for 10% of share purchases, mostly from Northern Ireland. A sample investigation of the ownership of 90 companies in the years 1933–1935 revealed that 9.3% of paid-up capital was owned by shareholders outside the state, which would represent investment by foreigners of approximately £550,000 during the years 1932–1936 (CBC 1938 evid. par. 97). Some investment, as in the case of Gentex textile firm or Waterford Ironfounders, took the form of secondhand equipment rather than finance, and some foreign capital probably hid behind Irish nominee shareholders. Irrespective of its composition, the sums were significant, though the flotation of Ranks (Ireland) resulted in substantial capital outflow to Britain.

Domestic funds came from a variety of resources including bank deposits, which fell by £12 million. The industrialization drive led to the formation of development committees, who mobilized the small savings of provincial towns, and resulted in many small first-time investors. The initial shareholders in the Portlaoise plant of Irish Worsted Mills included a cross section of the local community: doctors, widows, accountants, teachers, shopkeepers, shop assistants, nurses, an Electricity Supply Board driver and collector, engine drivers and railway porters, priests, and retired police officers. The local convent invested £75 (TID 19/145). Local capital reduced start-up costs and anchored outside businesses more firmly in the community. Vincent Crowley, who chaired Irish Tanners, insisted on holding the company's first annual general meeting in its hometown of Portlaw to give the local investors an opportunity of attending.[2]

While several issues were heavily oversubscribed, the patriotic urge to invest in the country's future was tempered by a desire for security. Preference shares in established companies and the subsidiaries of well-known British firms were favored. An issue of 20,000 preference shares in Fry-Cadbury (Ireland) Ltd. was heavily oversubscribed, a list for preference shares in Sunbeam Wolsey closed early due to oversubscription (*Ir. Ind. Yearbook* Oct. 1933; *IT* 11 Dec. 1934), and 175,000 Ranks *s*. Ordinary Shares were issued at a price of 15*s*. (CVO evid. doc. 69A). The value of some shares was boosted because few were available to the public: Dunlop and Sunbeam Wolsey offered only preference shares; only £131,000 of Ranks £1.3 million shares were on public offer, a pattern repeated by P. J. Carroll (F200/16/38). Established investors bought such blue-chip shares; one stockbroker's books show Ranks (Ireland) and Ever-Ready (Ireland) shares being added to portfolios containing government securities, Guinness, and leading British shares (Dublin Municipal Archives, B1/).

Such investments proved highly profitable, especially the shares of firms in a position to capitalize on their protected status such as Ranks, which benefited from the high flour prices set to ensure the viability of small mills. By 1935 Ranks yielded an annual 20%; other milling shares such as Bolands and Barrow Milling also paid high dividends. The shoe firm of J. H. Woodington, established as a private company with a new manufactures license, was floated on the stock exchange in 1936 at a price of £90,000, 50% above its physical asset value (which critics alleged represented the capitalized value of protection). At the same time, the Dublin pharmaceutical company May Roberts, with an annual turnover of £250,000, was capitalized at £175,000, of which £100,000 represented goodwill including the benefits of the package tax, though the ICC claimed that May Roberts was extremely profitable in 1930.

Many firms publicized the benefits of protection or monopoly to boost flotations. The prospectus for Irish Wire Products noted

2. Information supplied by Dr. Jeremiah Dempsey who was first secretary of Irish Tanners.

their 75% tariff and reproduced a letter from Lemass that stated that "the Minister will not be disposed to grant facilities . . . to any other firm or individual proposing to manufacture articles already being supplied by your company." A similar letter was contained in the prospectus for Irish Dunlop while Cement Ltd. noted the firm's control of import quotas (CVO evid. doc. 69a and pars. 4735–70).

Stock exchange activity was heavily dependent on government policy (CBC 1938 evid, pars. 11707–8), though a benevolent tariff regime did not ensure success. The financial record of many new companies was unimpressive, and few firms founded without the support of a foreign parent paid dividends on ordinary shares before 1939. The subscription list for Irish Tanners was heavily oversubscribed (*IT* 11 Dec. 1934), but no dividend was paid on ordinary shares until 1937 and then and for several years at the rate of 5%. Pressure to pay dividends, irrespective of commercial prospects, was high. When Irish Tanners applied for a price increase in August 1935, one official noted: "The Directors at Portlaw also want to ensure that a decent dividend will be payable to the shareholders. Apparently there is no intention of waiting till the business is a success but good dividends must be paid right away" (TID 43/63). A growing awareness of the poor return on many new shares deterred investment in subsequent new issues (CBC 1938 evid. p. 395), making it difficult to raise funds for unproven companies.

### The Industrial Credit Company

The state investment bank, the Industrial Credit Company, was responsible for underwriting more than 60% of issues between 1934 and 1939. In the years 1933–1935 the ICC underwrote three issues in excess of £500,000—Ranks, the Irish Sugar Company, and Irish Cement, all high-quality investments—and five for sums between £100,000–£200,000. In later years the quantity and quality of issues declined; only three issues were for sums in excess of £100,000 in the years 1936–1939, and the shares proved less attractive. The ICC was forced to take up over 35% of ordinary shares underwritten in the years 1935–1937, though debentures and preference shares remained popular (BP26290A). The company handled only eight issues in the years 1936–1939, compared with twenty-one in the years 1933–1935.

Although the establishment of an industrial credit company had been mooted by officials on several occasions during the Cumann na nGaedheal administration (McG Papers P35/b/20), it did not receive cabinet consideration until Fianna Fail came to power. In May 1932 J. P. Colbert, chairman of the state-controlled Agricultural Credit Company, proposed that the ACC provide credit for industry; however, a cabinet committee recommended a separate industrial credit organization (S6315; S6341). The committee proposed that share capital and directorships should be jointly held by the state and the banks with bank branches acting as agencies. The new body would provide direct advances, guarantees, underwriting of new issues, and investments in industry (S6467).

However, Lemass proposed that the banks concentrate on providing short-term capital and that a wholly state-owned company with a capital of £1 million be established to underwrite and hold shares in unproven Irish companies. Although he envisaged the possibility of heavy losses on some shares he emphasized that if the government wished to start "any industrial enterprise of doubtful possibilities . . . in the national interest" the capital should be secured by other means. This proposal received cabinet endorsement in March 1933 (Cab. C7/17) and was introduced to the Dail as a matter of urgency (S4871). The bill provided for a limited company with a capital value of £5 million. Shares were to be offered to the public with the minister for finance taking up the balance. MacEntee, the minister for finance, envisaged an extensive range of investments being financed by the new company such as mineral development, paper making, industrial alcohol, cement, and sugar beet. While all shares underwritten would be offered to the public, he anticipated a significant proportion remaining in ICC hands (PDDE 4 July 1933).

The company commenced business in December 1933. Of the initial £500,000 offered for public subscription only £7,936 was taken up, while a second issue of £500,000 offered in July 1936 attracted a mere £75 (CBC 1938, par. 427), perhaps because the ICC failed to pay a dividend until 1940. The commercial banks had expected a request to take up the shortfall but De Valera believed that they were not disposed to help the government's development

program, and the minister of finance reassured them that any subscription would be voluntary (BI, Irish Banks Standing Committee
minutes 31 March, 6 July 1933).

The absence of bank involvement, in contrast to the ACC, left
the ICC with greater operating freedom though lack of funds ruled
out the creation of a state holding company. Until 1936 it operated
with a capital value of £500,000; the 1936 issue of £500,000 was not
fully paid up so that the company's capital then amounted to
£812,500, a figure maintained for many years. Lack of capital meant
that the ICC provided little long-term finance for industry. By
October 1936 it had provided twelve loans amounting to a total of
£323,778, and only one loan, for £166,559 to the Irish Sugar Company, was for a substantial sum (CBC 1938, par. 434). ICC chairman
J. P. Colbert claimed that the majority of loan applications were "of
an unacceptable character," and the ICC discouraged trade loan
business preferring that firms apply to the commercial banks (B
Papers 26290A). The ICC's loan business may have been constrained
by an unwillingness to compete with the commercial banks, an
ambition that would appear to have been realized as, in contrast to
the ACC, there is no evidence that ICC was criticized by the Irish
Banks Standing Committee. However, it was criticized by the Banking Commission for its underwriting activities, and by the FII for
promoting "alien penetration."

The Banking Commission claimed that by beginning its underwriting with Ranks and the state-owned Irish Sugar Company the
ICC set unduly high expectations in terms of security and profitability, expectations that would not be met by newer companies. However, J. P. Beddy claimed that if the company had confined itself to
underwriting new projects its record would have been "a succession
of failures"; underwriting Ranks furthered the aim of establishing a
capital market for Irish industrial issues (CVO evid. doc. 66). The
commission criticized the company for underwriting smaller, more
speculative shares because the ICC, and indirectly the state, was left
holding a substantial proportion of shares in private industry—
though this had been originally envisaged. The commission argued
that alternative underwriting facilities would have been available
both for large and small issues. It recommended that the ICC's
capital be limited to £1 million, that it should be largely precluded

from borrowing funds and prevented from acting as an underwriter when holding borrowed funds (CBC 1938, par. 436–43).

However, it is doubtful whether as many shares could have been launched in the company's absence; the ICC underwrote in excess of 60% of all issues for the years 1934–1939, ranging from 83% in 1934 to 35% in the following year (B Papers 26290A). Those not underwritten by the ICC consisted of larger issues for cinemas, gas, Irish Shell, Independent Newspapers, and established firms such as P. J. Carroll and J. and L. F. Goodbody. Less than 5% of non-ICC underwritten issues related to new or unestablished firms[3]. The assertion that small issues would have found alternative support was refuted by ICC chairman Colbert who argued that "except in the case of the Slane Brick Co. (where the underwriters were unable to meet their engagements) no entirely new industrial proposition has been underwritten by any institution other than the ICC" (B Papers 26290A). ICC officials noted that their success had been responsible for attracting other underwriters into the field, such as the commercial banks and the New Ireland Assurance Company. They claimed that when they sought support from the stock exchange and issuing houses for their first major venture—the Sugar Company Debenture stock—"the making of a public issue was strongly deprecated, on the ground that it had an Industrial background, and failure was predicted for the Issue" (F200/16/38). The ICC's failure to pay a dividend until 1940 and then a modest 2.5% suggests that a company motivated by profit would have been unlikely to replace the state enterprise. By 1939 an investor with an equal amount in ICC-underwritten securities would have suffered a depreciation of 4.94% on his investment and would earn a gross dividend of 4.21% on stock; by the end of 1940 this hypothetical investor would have shown an appreciation of 3% with 5.12% on dividend (Industrial Credit Co. annual reports 1939, 1940), a record much inferior to the stock market as a whole.

A comparison between the ICC's performance and the ideas outlined by the minister for finance suggests that the company fulfilled its brief of launching new Irish industries. The criticism voiced by the Banking Commission suggests that certain individuals

3. Analysis derived from app. 5 of the Banking Commission report.

disapproved, notably Joseph Brennan, who drafted the critical para-graphs[4]. His hostility was shared by senior Finance officials. When Brennan queried why the company had been given a share capital of £5 million A. Bayne of Finance responded with a note stating that "Ministers devised the bill with the minimum of advice and assis-tance and prepared their own briefs" (BP 26290A). Brennan criti-cized the 6% return offered on preference shares for the Irish Sugar Company, criticism rejected by Colbert on the grounds that 6% "was barely sufficient to interest the Stock Exchange and attract the public" (BP 26349). Brennan argued that public companies were using their "privileged conditions" to raise capital by means of 6.5% preference shares, a practice that was "definitely prejudicial to the raising of capital on any moderate terms by business concerns that do not enjoy such favour" (BP 26350).

While Brennan's wish for a lower cost of capital is laudable, inexperienced Irish investors may have required a higher return than their British counterparts, and a unilateral policy by the ICC of providing a lower return on preference shares is unlikely to have succeeded. Preference shares issued by other underwriters for two established companies, Irish Cinemas Ltd. and James Crean and Son, carried 6% dividends, and most of the latter issue remained with the underwriter. ICC figures suggest that the weighted average return on preference shares in Dublin was 5.646% compared with 5.246% in London (F200/16/38).

The ICC was subjected to further criticism on the grounds that it underwrote foreign-controlled companies and furthered alien pen-etration. In 1935 the FII argued that the primary purpose of the ICC should be to finance industry "in the beneficial ownership of Saorstat nationals" (Daly 1984b, 266). In response, the ICC expressed its concern that the provisions of the Control of Manufactures Acts were observed "in the letter and in the spirit" but did not see it as the ICC's duty "to usurp the functions of the Oireachtas by going beyond these Acts to legislate privately for industrial promoters" (ICC an-nual report 1936). Beddy informed the Commission on Vocational Organisation "that if the Legislature passes an Act of Parliament which can be over-ridden we are powerless to prevent it being over-

4. BP 26290A contains a pencil draft of para. 442 and other key sections.

ridden. . . . There are devices which are resorted to by various people which enable them to get around the Act. We cannot stop them. It is done all the time" (CVO evid, qs 4725–26).

Companies underwritten by the ICC such as Ranks or Salts had their shareholding structured to comply with the Control of Manufactures Act. The ICC connived at such practices, as did Industry and Commerce, though the advice on how to comply was given by outside lawyers (often suggested by the ICC), most commonly Arthur Cox[5]. The ICC claimed that many businesses required "the co-operation of an external organisation" to ensure technical success and argued that these issues resulted "in placing into predominant Irish ownership and control businesses which were previously largely owned by outside interests" (ICC annual report 1936; CVO evid., doc. 66).

While outwardly the ICC remained unrepentant, public criticism was not without effect. In 1937, "in view of the allegations which had been recently made that his company was one of the agents for 'alien' penetration in Saorstat industries," Beddy sought Lemass's opinion on the proposed shareholding of a steel company, admitting that while "the arrangements complied technically with the Control of Manufactures Act, he felt it was open to objection in being opposed to the spirit of the Act" (TID 94/49).

Allegations of discrimination against Irish companies were a corollary of charges that the ICC was an agent of "foreign penetration." The Commission on Vocational Organisation was unable to determine the merits of the case but noted the existence of "sharply conflicting evidence on this point" (CVO par. 424). In evidence the ICC noted that it had received 89 underwriting proposals, 55 relating to new and 34 to established companies. Of the new applications, 24 were wholly Irish of which 12 were rejected, 4 because they were not manufacturing concerns, while 14 of 31 that were not exclusively Irish were rejected; however, J. J. Walsh alleged that of twenty new companies underwritten by the ICC only Arklow Pottery was wholly under Irish control (CVO evid. par 4920, doc. 66A). That the ICC promoted companies with substantial foreign participation is indisputable; this was inevitable given their bias towards large enter-

5. Information supplied by the ICC.

prises, most of which had substantial foreign participation. The attacks by Irish business interests reflect a general disenchantment with industrial policy and the ICC's apparent immunity from interest groups. Beddy affirmed their independence from ministerial intervention and emphasized that they had "turned down several propositions that were rather wished upon us," none of which subsequently proved successful.

The Commission on Vocational Organisation adopted a similarly neutral stance towards allegations that the ICC connived at the capitalization by firms of import quotas, tariff protection, or new manufactures licenses. Colbert emphasized that "we have turned down several propositions which mean cashing in on government post-1933 protection," though several prospectuses of shares underwritten by the ICC mentioned the company's protected position. The prospectus for the Ranks issue noted that the company held milling licenses and that they were transferable, though the ICC only accepted this inclusion following government approval (CVO evid. pars. 4694–4807).

The ICC could dismiss allegations of anti-Irish bias in the knowledge that they were part of an overall criticism of government policy; however, Banking Commission recommendations to limit ICC capital and to forbid underwriting while the company held borrowed funds gave rise to considerable concern. The commission's assessment was not fully accepted even within the Department of Finance. In July 1938 Finance noted that "the Commission has based its criticism of these organisations [ICC, etc.] on the somewhat narrow grounds of financial technique and it has not sufficiently appreciated the underlying circumstances which rendered the creation of these organisations necessary" and proposed that the recommendations be discussed with the departments primarily involved (S10612).

The ICC sought clarification of government policy on the grounds that its business was being impeded by uncertainty. However, no action was taken, and in April 1939 Industry and Commerce pressed for a statement rejecting the recommendations of the Banking Commission respecting the ICC. The department argued that in the absence of the ICC, the state would have been forced to supply £7.5 million of capital for industrial development and that the capital market developed by the ICC remained essential to government policy. However, MacEntee wrote to De Valera opposing such a statement, and the matter remained in limbo (S11244) with the ICC seriously short of capital and consequently vulnerable, which was possibly a deliberate Finance ploy. World War II relieved the ICC of its immediate problems; underwriting was deferred, and share buoyancy boosted its investments and postponed the debate over its future.

The ICC claimed to operate independently of government departments, instituting its own examination of company proposals, examining prospective markets and production costs, and liaising with commercial banks on an applicant's financial standing.[6] This independence gave rise to concern in Finance in 1934 when it was feared that the ICC would support firms that would compete with existing firms "to a point beyond the known capacity of the market," and arrangements were instituted to prevent such an occurrence (F97/2/34). The ICC advised companies on choosing directors and recommended strategies in times of difficulty but do not appear to have used shareholdings to influence policy. While the prospect of establishing a state holding company similar to the Italian IRI (Institute per la Ricostruzioni Industriale [Institute for Industrial Reconstruction]) was briefly mooted, such an option was precluded by shortage of finance, though proposals prepared by Industry and Commerce in 1943 envisaged the ICC exploring and preparing new industrial projects and promoting the establishment of new companies which it would finance (S11987A).

*Trade Loans*

The March 1933 paper on industrial credit drafted by Sean Lemass envisaged the ICC as part of a three-pronged approach. Short-term credit was the preserve of the commercial banks, while a letter from the Irish Banks Standing Committee in October 1932 announced their willingness to become actively involved in the provision of longer-term industrial finance through the trade loans guarantee scheme, offering funds at an interest rate 0.5% below bank rate. This

6. Information supplied by Frank Casey, managing director of the ICC.

decision was in marked contrast to the banks' opposition in earlier years and reflected an awareness that the trade loans scheme was smaller and less of a threat than had been feared, coupled perhaps with the impact of a depression that made it difficult to overlook secure investments (S6467). In 1933 the Committee on Industrial Finance recommended that trade loans legislation should be extended until the ICC was in operation. However on 20 March 1933 the executive council extended the measure for a further five years, increased the finance available by £1 million, and removed the restriction forbidding loans for working capital. Funds had already been made available for house building, and guarantees were extended to small businesses (Daly 1984a, 85).

Despite this extension trade loans were viewed as a temporary measure (PDDE 4 July 1933). In practice a total of 78 guarantees were issued during the years 1932–1937, amounting to almost £600,000, the majority for sums less than £10,000. In 1936 firms assisted by trade loans were alleged to have generated 5,790 jobs compared with 674 in 1931 (F97/3/38). The post-1932 loans were substantially more successful than earlier ventures, with only £14,500 in default by 1937, because of the greater profitability of protected markets. While several loans were issued for large amounts—notably £90,000 for bog development—most were for modest sums directed to small industries. This pattern may reflect the wishes of Lemass who told the Dail in 1933 that he envisaged trade loans as assisting companies too small to have recourse to the public capital market (Daly 1984a, 86). Trade loans were complementary to the ICC rather than in competition—an Irish solution to the "Macmillan gap"[7].

Despite an improved success rate the scheme was subjected to considerable criticism by the Banking Commission, notably from McElligott. The commission's 1938 report repeated the recommendations of the 1926 Banking Commission that the restrictions imposed in the original legislation "shall be carefully and rigidly insisted on" and emphasized that "the Government should not seek to deal

---

7. So-called because the "gap," the shortage of financial institutions lending to companies too small to borrow on the stock exchange, was first identified by the British government's Committee on Finance and Industry (1931 Cmd 3897) chaired by Lord Macmillan.

directly with individual businesses in providing assistance for long-term credit." It recommended that state provision for long-term credit should be handled not by a government department, as in the case of Trade Loans, but by the Industrial Credit Company. That the legislation was due to lapse in 1938 lent urgency to these recommendations.

The possibility of establishing a small loans section within the ICC was considered but opposed by Lemass on the grounds that the majority of applicants would be rejected because of inadequate security. Lemass pressed for their continuation, seeing trade loans as an instrument of regional policy, and his will prevailed against the objection of Finance and less than wholehearted support from Leydon, in part because of the existence of superior government loan facilities in Northern Ireland (F97/3/38). Lemass welcomed having trade loans under his direct control, granted on the recommendations of advisory committees.

*Conclusions*

While the financial sector was affected by the new economic regime, its fundamental institutions remained unscathed, and the country's banks and currency remained independent of government authority. Despite a deterioration in the balance of payments and some decline in external investments held by Irish residents, the country's creditor position remained intact, and in 1939 she was one of "less than ten creditor nations in the world," with an excess of sterling assets over liabilities in the banks of £63.5 million (F39/5/39). Fianna Fail failed to channel external investments into domestic outlets as Lemass had urged while in opposition, and this was also true of insurance funds.

The major changes related to the Dublin capital market with the establishment of the ICC and the rising volume and value of transactions, especially in industrial companies. Some of this was in response to more profitable investment opportunities and would have occurred independent of further government initiatives but the ICC played a major role.

The restraint of Fianna Fail intervention in the financial sector is of considerable significance. There was no effort to establish a state holding company; ICC shareholdings resulted from the reluctance of private investors rather than from defined policy, and the long-term aim was the encouragement of private shareholding rather than state investment. A more active state financial policy involving tapping commercial banks for investment funds or gaining control over the country's external assets could have funded investments such as cement or an oil refinery without the danger of foreign control. However, such proposals were never mooted, and while Lemass proved eager to control exports, he never expressed similar designs on the banking system.

Further, perhaps conclusive evidence of Fianna Fail conservatism is provided by the Banking Commission, a body dominated by banking interests and the Department of Finance, whose advocacy of the status quo and criticism of government policy cannot have been unexpected. Its main function appears to have been the destruction of those groups advocating the unorthodox financial ideas of Major Douglas such as a currency backed by social credit. Such ideas were not without support in sections of Fianna Fail; among supporters was Frank Aiken, minister for defense. However, given the apparent, if unvoiced, opposition of De Valera, Lemass, and MacEntee, they were doomed to failure, while alternatives such as Keynesianism were not considered.

# 8 The 1938 Anglo-Irish Trade Agreement
## A New Equilibrium

THE 1938 TRADE AGREEMENT marks the end of the economic war with Britain and of the attempt to bring about a self-sufficient Ireland. The economic war that began in 1932 is often regarded as the driving force behind the self-sufficiency policy. The dispute over financial payments was part of a broader constitutional disagreement, and the deterioration in Anglo-Irish relations owed more to De Valera's wish to dismantle the 1921 treaty than to a failure to repay monies owed. Britain realized that the annuities issue was the weakest part of its case against Ireland (Canning 1987, 132). Both countries sacrificed economic interests for political ends, with constitutional issues taking precedence over a trade and financial settlement (McMahon 1984, 197).

While the economic war exerted a major influence on Irish economic policy, it was not the determining factor. The self-sufficiency program predated the dispute, and the Irish government had imposed numerous duties prior to the outbreak of the economic war, though British imports were subject to a preferential rate. Ireland was not the first dominion to embark on a program of protection. The Australian state of Victoria introduced tariffs as early as 1866; Canada followed suit in 1878 (Butlin 1959; Aitken 1959), as did South Africa and New Zealand in later years. However, these countries had never been an integral part of the U.K. economy, and by the 1930s their protection had the sanction of tradition. The Irish shift occurred within a context of hostile political relations at a time when Britain had begun to support domestic agriculture.

Anglo-Irish trading relations would have been strained in the absence of a political dispute. The Fianna Fail election manifesto expressed the intention of retaining close economic relations with Britain while building up protected industry by giving Britain preference in purchases of capital goods and machinery in return for preferential treatment for Irish agricultural exports (Moynihan 1980, 190). This state of affairs would not have satisfied Britain, which was trying to accommodate closer trading relations with the dominions within the ambit of protection and had embarked on negotiations leading to the Imperial Trade Conference at Ottawa in the summer of 1932. The response to the tariffs imposed in the Irish budget was a statement that there was "no point in the planned trade discussions in preparation for Ottawa" (Canning 1987, 132).

While the Irish delegation was en route to Ottawa in July 1932, the economic war broke out when Britain imposed special duties on Irish exports in retaliation for Ireland's default on annuity payments. In response the Irish government imposed emergency duties on imports of British coal, cement, sugar, electrical machinery, and iron and steel: one-third of imports from Britain (Kennedy, Giblin, and McHugh 1988, 42). These remained the only Irish duties imposed because of the economic war, though British imports lost their preferential rates. Britain and Ireland failed to sign a trade agreement at Ottawa though discussions took place that may have been halted by De Valera's opposition (McMahon 1984, 50–79). In consequence Irish goods became liable for duties imposed under the 1932 Import Duties Act in addition to special duties (McG Papers P35/b/44).

While the major burden of the economic war fell on agriculture, the crisis did not aid industry. With the exception of sugar, emergency duties hit imports that were essential to industrial development. De Valera's persistence in the dispute in the teeth of opposition from MacEntee and Lemass, the key economics ministers, belies the belief that he engineered the economic war in order to realize his "drastic experiment in economic nationalism" (Hancock 1937, 350). Agricultural self-sufficiency would have been better realized if the government had not been burdened with export subsidies consequent on British duties. De Valera made repeated references to the economic war in an effort to encourage a sense of national solidarity; whether this was essential to the support of protection we cannot say. Kennedy, Giblin, and McHugh, like Hancock, doubt whether De Valera could have persisted with his policy, particularly "material frugality," in the absence of the economic war (1988, 41). Yet without it there would have been less frugality. Appeals to patriotism did little to curb imports. One Cork radio manufacturer claimed that "to talk of patriotism to the local wireless dealer or wireless user is to fool oneself. The price in most cases is what matters and it is immaterial if the battery is made in Timbuctoo" (TID 1207/107).

Agricultural prices showed a severe decline, attributable in part to international depression, but the widening gap between store cattle prices in the Irish Free State and those in Northern Ireland (they had been virtually identical prior to 1932) shows that other factors were at work.[1] Before 1932 British and Irish wholesale agricultural prices moved in unison; by 1936 Irish prices were 37% below 1929 levels compared to 24% for British prices (S9420). However, Britain's switch to agricultural protection would have denied Irish farmers British price levels in the absence of the economic war. The volume of British agricultural imports fell during the thirties, with the most pronounced fall occurring in live cattle, Ireland's major export. British cattle prices fell sharply during the years 1932–1933 when many animals could not be sold (Whetham 1976, 44–45). By 1934 Irish cattle imports were subject to heavy specific duties and stringent quotas, which Britain claimed were a result of agricultural policy rather than of the economic war (Kennedy, Giblin, and McHugh 1988, 210–11, 42).

Britain failed to reach agreement over meat with "friendly" dominions, and Australia was forced to observe "voluntary" restrictions on meat exports to Britain (Drummond 1974, 307). Access for agricultural imports was directly related to concessions for British exports. Denmark negotiated a trade agreement in 1933 permitting duty-free pigmeat exports in return for importing British coal.

1. In 1932 Irish store prices avraged £12.39m, those in Northern Ireland £12.15; by 1933 the Irish figure was £8.96, Northern Ireland's £11.02; by 1934, Ireland was at £6.86, Northern Ireland, £10.58 (Neary and O'Grada 1986, 17).

Despite this agreement, Danish agricultural output was virtually stationery throughout the thirties; agricultural prices fell more sharply than in Ireland, and the government was forced to introduce similar support schemes (Jorberg and Kuntz, 1976, 400–402; Johansen 1987, 47–52). The price for free access for Irish agricultural produce would have been no extension of tariffs, though even this step might not have been sufficient to deter British farmers from pressing for restrictions on Irish farm imports.

Walter Layton, editor of the *Economist,* claimed that the British tariff war against Ireland had been undertaken either to foment a coup against Fianna Fail or "more probably, in order to satisfy the insistent clamour of English agriculture" (Canning 1987, 154). Lemass countered claims that all farmers' woes could be attributed to the economic war by referring to the protests from British farmers when a settlement appeared to be in sight, while the Northern Ireland government voiced vigorous protests against the 1935 coal-cattle pact, which marked the first thaw in the dispute (McMahon 1984, 152). A memorandum by the Irish Department of Agriculture in 1947 noted that the economic war had facilitated British measures to increase cattle output but did not cause them (S9420).

Ireland's share of British imports declined for all agricultural commodities (Kennedy, Giblin, and McHugh 1988, 212) because of the economic war, and most of the cost of British special duties was borne by Irish agriculture (Neary and O'Grada 1986, 14). Bilateral trade agreements with countries such as Germany brought little benefit, though they galvanized Britain into the first coal-cattle pact. In 1936 exports to other countries amounted to £1.8 million compared with £19.8 million to Britain and Northern Ireland; farm exports to non-British markets amounted to half the additional trade secured by the coal-cattle agreement (S9420).

While Irish protectionism did not cause the dispute, Britain came to regard a modification of Irish tariffs and quotas as essential to any settlement, just as the country sought similar concessions from other dominions. British economic interests were propelled towards conciliation by the depressed state of the coal industry and by the consequences of Irish industrialization. In January 1933 a British interdepartmental committee emphasized that Britain would require abolition of Irish emergency duties, restoration of U.K. preference, modification of duties, and an end to import licenses and other controls as part of any settlement. It urged linking financial and trade agreements on the grounds that "if any concessions are made on the land annuities question we should be in a better position to secure compensatory benefits in the trade sphere" (McMahon 1984, 107). In 1935, the Treasury's chief economic advisor, Horace Wilson, urged the need for a trade and financial agreement "if the growing movement in the Irish Free State to set up more factories is to be countered before it is too late" (T160/744; F14026/1). Irish priorities lay in achieving optimum access for agricultural exports, for which Britain would require a quid pro quo.

Initial negotiations concentrated on areas that did not conflict with Irish protectionism. The coal-cattle pacts from 1935, where Ireland contracted to buy more British coal in return for increased cattle exports, are a case in point. In 1936 Leydon offered to channel to Britain orders for cement factory equipment and capital equipment for the Electricity Supply Board (ESB) and hinted that Ireland could impose tariffs on certain foreign imports, giving a market advantage to Britain. British officials viewed such concessions as of limited value because, as a result of the secrecy surrounding Irish import licenses, they could not be "put in front of the shop window." They pressed for concessions on the package tax, minimum customs duties, and imports of cotton thread and cloths (T160/744; F14026/2), items at the heart of the Irish protectionist program, though these were rejected. The 1936 agreement provided for increased imports of Irish fat cattle and reduced duties on other agricultural produce. In return Ireland granted concessions on coal and cement imports, reduced emergency duties by 10%, and agreed to refrain from influencing importers against the purchase of British goods, though they requested that this final concession not be mentioned because of political sensitivity (T160/744; F14026/3).

The ratification of Ireland's 1937 Constitution, the accession of Neville Chamberlain as prime minister, and worsening international relations all improved the prospects for settlement. By 1938 revenue from British special duties was expected to equal the sum owed in annuities, and the inability to find alternative markets for Irish agriculture was generally accepted. Much of the gloss was fading off the Fianna Fail economic program. It had failed to halt the drift of population to Dublin and Britain, and small farmers were not deriving the anticipated benefits from agricultural schemes. A return to more traditional policies was gaining favor.

A report on trade relations with Britain dated December 1936, signed by the secretaries of the Departments of Agriculture, Industry and Commerce, Finance, and External Affairs, harked back to Cumann na nGaedheal economic policy. It asserted that a settlement and a healthier agriculture would raise farm incomes, employ more farm laborers, halt the drift to the towns, and lead to increased industrial employment, while the "restoration of public confidence" would reduce interest rates, permitting cheaper funding of housing and public works, and would attract the return of wealthy tax-paying residents. This analysis, which represented the reinvigoration of the "Finance mind," was similar to that being carried out by the Banking Commission. Both pointed towards an end to the dispute and towards concessions on protection. However, while the report was signed by all four secretaries, twelve months later MacEntee, the finance minister, informed De Valera that "a marked difference of opinion" existed between them on the merits of seeking major trading concessions from Britain or minor modifications and sought De Valera's advice (S9420).

The ensuing trade talks suggest that both strategies were attempted: Ireland began by offering minor alterations but moved to more fundamental concessions. From the outset of the 1938 negotiations, which included talks on British naval bases in Ireland, Britain set out to link a financial agreement with concessions on trade. The opening statements from De Valera and Lemass offered Britain little more than the prospect of supplying capital equipment to Irish industry and a possibility of preferential duties that would enable her to capture a greater share of (static) Irish imports.

When British and Irish officials reviewed progress on 31 January after two weeks of negotiations, British officials protested that the only concessions offered by Ireland applied to cellulose wrapping and iron and steel goods, imports amounting to a mere £22,000, plus an offer of duty-free access for Britain, with tariffs imposed on competitors, for a range of imports then worth £8 million (£3 million of this coal), which Britain saw as purely temporary pending the extension of Irish industry. While Leydon admitted that the concessions were "not of any great magnitude," he emphasized that his aim was to restore Britain's percentage share of Irish imports to its pre-1932 level. He reiterated Ireland's need for protection because her industry was "in the cradle," and prices in consequence were high.

This statement caused T. G. Jenkins, who led the Board of Trade delegation, to suggest that there was "a very great difference between duties to equalise prices (even considering the high Cost of Production) and the prohibitive duties which were so common in the Eire tariff." He suggested that the Irish government reduce duties to a level that would permit British manufactures to compete "on level terms having regard to differences in costs of production," a concession identical to that given by other dominions at Ottawa. Jenkins proposed that Ireland establish a tariff board on the Australian or Canadian model to review or conventionalize duties.

Leydon appears to have responded positively to these suggestions. In the course of informal discussions after the meeting, he informed British officials of his plans to fly to Dublin and claimed that his intention was "to press his minister to agree to a drastic reconstruction of the Eire protective system, so that the present high protection, either by quota or duty, should be replaced by a protection only sufficient to offset the higher cost of production in Eire as against the United Kingdom and consequently to give United Kingdom goods a chance of competition in the market." He sought reassurance that such concessions on Ireland's part would be matched by dominion-type trading conditions for Irish imports, and this was given informally some hours later (BT11/2832). On 3 February the Irish cabinet agreed that discussions might proceed on this basis (G.C.1/7a). Britain was informed of Ireland's offer to establish a Prices Commission similar to those in Australia and Canada in return for dominion-style status for Irish imports (BT11/2832), and this formed the core of the 1938 agreement.

The Irish concession gave rise to mixed responses from British officials. Its main author, T. G. Jenkins, stated that it "virtually amounted to a complete reversal of the original basis of negotiations laid down by Eire ministers"; a Treasury official believed that the agreement would arouse considerable alarm in Northern Ireland and feared that the prospect of increased Irish food imports would force a reduction in British farm prices and consequent pressure for subsidies. Some weeks later he announced that "the Settlement amounted to an unfavourable agreement on Defence; an unfavourable agreement on Finance and an unfavourable agreement on Trade." Another official noted the "wholly illogical" fact that while Britain gave immediate concessions to Irish trade, Britain received in return a promise to submit Irish duties to examination by a Prices Commission—a model that had "unfortunately worked very badly" from the British point of view in the Australian and Canadian cases. However, he concluded that the merits of the agreement "must be judged largely on general political and economic grounds" (T160/746; F4026/03/3).

Negotiations moved to matters of detail with the greatest controversy relating to requests for special treatment for imports from Northern Ireland and the composition of the free list, a list of goods that the Irish undertook not to protect. De Valera used the negotiations to present partition as a central issue in Anglo-Irish relations, while the possibility of an agreement led to protests from Northern Ireland politicians. Britain urged the Irish Free State to accord special trading concessions to Northern Ireland both as a gesture of conciliation and to stem protests. However, De Valera argued that such a concession would give Northern Ireland the "best of both worlds"—partition plus a favorable opportunity of expanding its trade in Eire, opening the floodgates to intensive competition that would be highly prejudicial, if not disastrous to Eire's industries. Lemass expressed the fear that such concessions would mean the closure of twenty or more subsidiaries of Northern Ireland plants, the end of self-sufficiency, and the repeal of controls on foreign industries, and that industries would migrate to Northern Ireland, which had less onerous legislation on working conditions and hours of labor.

However, Chamberlain believed that if the only objections to a differential tariff were of an economic character, they would not have presented insuperable difficulties (Cab. 27/642). A subsequent proposal for progressive reductions in duties on Northern Ireland imports and free trade within five years was dismissed by Lemass on the grounds that it would be difficult to justify a provision giving duty-free entry to Northern Ireland goods "no matter what political

provocation the northern state might be guilty of at that time"
(BT11/2833). No concessions were made for Northern Ireland imports, and this proposal does not appear to have surfaced in postwar
negotiations.

The Anglo-Irish Trade Agreement was signed on 25 April
1938, one of three agreements signed on that day. One removed the
remaining British naval bases in Ireland. The financial agreement
resolved the dispute over annuities with a lump-sum payment of £10
million and removed the emergency duties imposed by both states.
Under the trade agreement, which was to run for three years and to
continue thereafter subject to six months' notice of termination, all
goods produced or manufactured in Ireland that were free of duty on
that date or were liable to either the 1932 Import Duties Act or
Ottawa duties would be admitted free of duty into Britain. Products
that had been subject to both Ottawa and Industrial Development
Act imposts—game, poultry, and dairy products—were only guaranteed duty-free entry until August 1940.

In common with other commonwealth countries, Irish dairy
and poultry produce were guaranteed a specified margin of preference
over the produce of noncommonwealth countries; however, whereas
countries with Ottawa agreements were guaranteed this in perpetu-
ity, Ireland's preference lasted only as long as Irish poultry and dairy
produce were permitted duty-free access. These clauses reflected
British reluctance to permit unrestricted access of Irish poultry and
dairy produce. British poultry producers were highly agitated about
the proposed agreement and Northern Ireland farmers appeared
vulnerable to increased competition. The British Ministry of Agriculture sought quotas on Irish poultry imports; however, the Board
of Trade felt that it would be "dangerous" to single out imports from
one empire country in this manner. James Ryan, Irish minister for
agriculture, was insistent on free entry for poultry on the grounds
that it would prove "politically impossible to return with an Agreement which did not give them concessions of free entry while free
entry obtained for more substantial cattle raising" (BT11/2833;
T160/746; F14026/03/5).

Britain agreed to only regulate Irish poultry and dairy imports
in the event of a failure by both sides to assure "orderly marketing."
In return Ireland granted Britain preferential terms on existing and

future tariffs—coal, motor parts, and motor cars were singled out for special concessions—and undertook to tax silk and artificial silk imports from other countries while British goods would be admitted duty-free. Britain was granted modest concessions on the package tax, and the level of minimum customs duty was reduced for British goods.

The above clauses proved relatively uncontentious from the Irish point of view, though Lemass informed the Dail that the provisions for importing motor parts would be welcomed by everybody except him (PDDE 28 Apr. 1938). The remaining clauses proved more controversial. Article 5 provided that imports from Britain of items on the free list were guaranteed entry free of duties (other than package tax) and quotas, while article 8 provided for the establishment of a Prices Commission to review protection and to substitute tariffs for quotas (McG Papers P35/b/44). Initially the free list proved less contentious than the Prices Commission though Lemass opposed the concept during negotiations on the grounds that it would prove difficult to remove an industry from the list. The question of whether to include iron and steel goods was highly contentious with Lemass arguing that pending the establishment of the Hawbowline plant they should be omitted and the British Iron and Steel Federation demanding an assurance of no new duties and preferential status (BT11/2833). The free list amounted to more than six pages of items covering 16.5% of Irish imports.

The clause that aroused most interest was the requirement to establish a tariff review procedure to which British industrial interests would have access via the Irish Prices Commission. In February 1938, Malcolm McDonald, the dominions secretary, informed an Irish delegation that "the undertaking regarding the Prices Commission was the crux of the agreement so far as the U.K. was concerned" (BT11/2833). In November 1938, W. B. Spender, Northern Ireland finance minister, claimed that since the agreement was signed imports to the Irish Free State from Britain had fallen by 9.6% and those from Northern Ireland by 14%, while Irish exports to Britain had risen by 12% and to Northern Ireland by 24%, ending, "So much for your Trade agreement. I hope we have done a little better with the U.S.A." However, the Board of Trade argued that it was impossible to reach any definite conclusion until the Prices Commission had issued a substantial number of reports (T160/746; F14026/03/5).

The 1938 trade agreement looked significantly more threatening to Irish protection than it proved in practice. The lengthy negotiations led to a substantial reduction in factory orders in anticipation of tariff reductions (FIM annual report 1938). News of the signing led to what Lemass described as "the almost complete cessation of trading" (PDDE 28 Apr. 1938). Reports that tariffs on shoes would fall to 20% led to threatened shutdowns and plant layoffs. The reaction was excessive, as quotas would continue until the Prices Commission ruled to the contrary, and higher tariffs could be substituted for abolished quotas.

The industrial clauses aroused widespread opposition. Patrick McGilligan claimed that the agreement had restored Irish trade to the 1932 situation with the important qualification that trade was now "hampered by an Agreement, the full extent of which has not yet been interpreted." The prospect of a strengthened Prices Commission was described by Labour T.D. W. Norton as "brimful of dangerous possibilities," and other opposition members regarded it as limiting Irish freedom to promote industrial development (PDDE 27–29 Apr. 1938).

Lemass pointed out that similar clauses had been imposed on Canada and New Zealand in the course of the Ottawa agreements, and that the Canadian conditions were more onerous in that the review procedure covered both new and existing tariffs whereas the Anglo-Irish agreement only covered existing duties. Lemass claimed, perhaps disingenuously, to welcome the review, arguing that it had never been the intention to continue the high level of duties indefinitely, though the only speech he could cite in support of this position was one made on 31 January 1938, following the inception of the Anglo-Irish talks (PDDE 28 Apr. 1938).

The second reading of the Prices Commission (extension of functions) bill came before the Dail on 4 May, less than one week after the debate on the Anglo-Irish agreements, and the commission issued the first statutory notices that it was undertaking reviews on 10 June 1938. Between June 1938 and December 1940, fifty references were made to the Prices Commission at the request of the U. K. trade commissioner, covering 74 customs duties out of a total of approximately 350—a figure that includes purely revenue duties.

The need to make submissions raised the question of whether they would be made on behalf of an individual firm or the industrial sector as a whole. The president of the Federation of Irish Manufacturers (FIM) felt that the federation should represent all cases and proposed the establishment of an Industrial Bureau. However, this initiative collapsed in the face of conflicting interests between individual industries and because of a refusal to amend the federation's constitution to permit the admission of all foreign firms (FIM minutes 10 June 1938, 6 Jan. 1939).

The federation's self-confidence was shattered by the announcement in June 1938 that prices would also be examined in four cases. FIM viewed this as an attack on Irish manufacturers "both by British interests and also by wholesalers and retailers and other manufacturers" (FIM minutes 17 June 1938). A deputation to the Prices Commission was allegedly placated with the information that its first finding would deal with an article for which a tariff could be justified, in order to reassure the public; however, by January 1939 the federation complained that the first announcement concerned an article with an excessive duty (FIM minutes 6 Jan. 1939), perhaps to placate British public opinion.

In practice the Prices Commission proved less threatening than it initially appeared, and this would have been evident from its inception to anyone with a knowledge of the Australian or Canadian equivalents (Drummond 1974, 390–420). The majority of reviews requested by the British authorities were never carried out. A mere fifteen reports were made between December 1938 and April 1941 when reviews were suspended owing to wartime concern with profiteering. The commission discharged thirteen references completely and two partially; seven were withdrawn at the request of the U.K. trade commissioner, as were parts of six further references. Thus the practical outcome of the Prices Commission amounted to quota and tariff modifications for soap and candles (McG Papers P35/b/44) and the introduction of a 75% tariff (50% preference for U.K. and Canada) in place of a 50% duty on manuscript books (ITJ Dec. 1939).

Unfortunately we know little of the workings of the commission. Irish files were destroyed in 1950,[2] while it appears that the

2. Information from the then Department of Trade, Commerce, and Tourism in 1983.

relevant British records were victims of wartime "floods and destruction." This makes it difficult to assess British reactions, though two contradictory comments survive. One Board of Trade official in 1951 noted that "judging from what few papers remain" the reviews carried out in 1939–1940 were "satisfactory"; however, in 1950 another official noted a reluctance on the part of the U.K. Trade Association to engage in a new round of Irish tariff reviews, this time under the auspices of the Industrial Development Authority. "As far as we are concerned the dog won't fight. They were so harassed by the Prices Commission before the War that they are more than reluctant to go through a similar experience again with the I.D.A." The nature of the harassment remains unspecified, though later references to "the type of exhaustive inquisition" (BT11/4410) suggest that Irish officials may have resorted to excessive bureaucratic demands on those petitioning for tariff reductions, a practice well established in the Tariff Commission of the twenties.

Excessive bureaucracy or an appreciation of common interests led British and Irish manufacturers to reach mutual agreements outside the ambit of the Prices Commission, something that neither government had contemplated. The Federation of Irish Manufacturers (FIM) Annual Report in 1940 noted that "it was found in some cases far more profitable to negotiate directly with the English Group concerned than to go through the lengthy and expensive procedure involved in a Prices Commission Examination." The implications of such collusion require further study.

The absence of records makes it impossible to gauge whether the Irish government was sincere in its intentions of using the commission to establish a more competitive industrial system, but there are grounds for scepticism. In March 1939 the FIM proposed to Industry and Commerce that a Dumping Commission be established, consisting of three representatives of each industry group, appointed by the federation, to guarantee against dumping by comparing prices of imported goods with those in the country of origin. Tariffs would be based on prices in country of origin rather than at point of import. They argued that the proposal offered the prospect of apparently lower tariffs and more effective protection. The proposal must be seen as a means of averting the potential threat posed by the Prices Commission.

Industry and Commerce welcomed it and suggested establishing an informal committee, which may indicate less than total sympathy with the Prices Commission, or alternatively a wish to soothe the ruffled feathers of Irish manufacturers. Finance showed outright hostility. McElligott viewed it as another example of the "scant courtesy" that Industry and Commerce showed Finance in submitting proposals for tariffs and suggested that they first establish that dumping had occurred. Efforts to persuade Finance to reconsider its objections proved futile, and the idea died with the outbreak of war (F200/4/39). However, the support shown by Industry and Commerce, together with the Prices Commission's dismissal of the overwhelming majority of cases and the apparent collusion between British and Irish industrialists suggests that there would not have been a surge of competition in the absence of war.

Despite the apparent negating of the immediate practical effects, Irish industry retained a bitter hostility towards the 1938 agreement. In 1948 a memorandum prepared by Kevin McCourt, secretary of the Federation of Irish Manufacturers, argued that the free list constituted "a hazard the industrialist cannot ignore," one that placed "a definite restriction" on the establishment of new industries. McCourt was equally vocal on the difficulties of reconciling the continuance of "adequate protection" for Irish industry while affording "full opportunities of reasonable competition" to British manufacturers, as the Prices Commission required. He objected to the requirement that reviews would result in the removal of quotas "irrespective of the conditions obtaining in this country and in the industry concerned and without regard to the capacity of British manufacturers to flood the Irish market with surplus goods" and expressed fears that comparisons of British and Irish costs would fail to take account of comparative taxes and markets (McG Papers P35/b/44).

In the long run, the Irish government was less exercised by tariff reviews than by the restrictions imposed by the free list. A memorandum from Industry and Commerce in 1947 prepared for the Anglo-Irish trade talks sought an end to the free list on the grounds that it caused major difficulties for officials attempting to negotiate the establishment of new industries. No criticism was voiced about tariff reviews; the memorandum quoted the policy of the minister for industry and commerce that protection would not be given to support an inefficient plant or management but only to offset labor costs higher than those prevailing elsewhere—wording almost identical to the 1938 agreement. This stance is in line with Lemass's abortive 1947 industrial efficiency bill, but it also reflects the negligible impact of tariff reviews. A further memorandum in February 1948 from Industry and Commerce noted that the possibility of price and tariff reviews at Britain's behest "helped to ensure that the Irish consumer would not be exploited by Irish manufacturers" (TID 555/12).

Postwar hostility to the 1938 agreement reflected the widening trade gap between Britain and Ireland. By 1948 a British Board of Trade official saw the agreement as resulting in £80 million of U.K. exports to Ireland and £30 million in Irish exports to Britain (BT11/8821); however, this imbalance reflects postwar trading patterns. Figures for the period from the agreement to the outbreak of war show that Irish imports from Britain and Northern Ireland increased from £22 million or 50% of total imports in 1937 to £24 million or 55.6% in 1939; imports stood at £44 million in 1937 and £43.4 million in 1939. Irish exports to Britain and Northern Ireland increased from £20 million or 90.6% of total exports in 1937 to £24.8 million or 93.6% in 1939, with exports rising from £22.2 million to £26.5 million in 1939 (McG Papers P35/b/44).

Contrary to the assertion of F. S. L. Lyons, "the basic principle" of the 1938 agreement was not "that of a return to the pre-1932 position" (Lyons 1973, 614). While the 1938 agreement reasserted the primacy of the export-oriented cattle sector at the expense of the commitment towards self-sufficiency and extensive farming, it proved less critical for Irish industrial interests, despite the initial panic. Assuming that suspicions of Irish efforts to negate the Prices Commission are correct, the free list provided a greater threat to extending protection. However the agreement was initially intended to last three years; we cannot know what form it might have taken in the absence of war.

### Conclusion

What emerged in 1938 was the accommodation of two superficially contradictory sets of vested interests: export-oriented Irish farmers, especially cattle farmers, and protected industrialists. The former recovered their traditional access to the British market on the best terms available given Britain's policy of promoting domestic agriculture, while the latter were not forced to cede industrial protection. Irish agriculture retained the price support systems instituted during the thirties for pork, grain, and dairy products. This new alignment of agricultural and industrial interests survived from 1938, with inevitable wartime disruptions, until the mid-fifties. It marks a synthesis or compromise with the previous economic history of the new state: the commitment of Cumann na nGaedheal to export-oriented agriculture and industry with minimal government assistance; the 1932 reversal of this stance with protection and self-sufficiency dominating both sectors. It is no coincidence that 1938 marked the end of serious ideological divisions between Ireland's major political parties on economic issues and on questions of national status; both Fianna Fail and Fine Gael broadly endorsed the 1938 compromise and continued it, with modifications, in the post-war period.

The 1938 agreement should therefore be deemed an Irish victory: concrete gains in terms of ports and an annuities settlement were not wiped out by the trade agreement, and the overall package brought consensus among the dominant forces in Irish politics and society. This consensus marked the end of Fianna Fail economic radicalism, demonstrated by the 1938 founding of Clann na Talmhan, a party representing small farmers of the west. Although token gestures continued to be made to small farmers, in 1938 the dominance of cattle farming was restored. Changes in industrial policy proved less fundamental: ideals of self-sufficiency, native control, female employment, and decentralization of industry remained dominant despite the evident shortcomings in achievement, though they now served to bolster entrenched interests rather than to spearhead a potentially radical agenda.

# 9 Conclusion

THE DECADES immediately following independence were marked by efforts to define a distinct Irish identity in political, cultural, and economic spheres (Foster 516, 1988). The process was marked by tension between the ill-defined ideals of the cultural and revolutionary nationalists and the realities of life in twentieth century Ireland. However, the ensuing compromises were rarely formally announced; instead a gulf frequently opened between rhetoric and reality, and historians writing on issues such as partition or the Irish language refer to "ambiguity," "contradictions" (O'Halloran 1987), or "schizophrenic attitudes" (T. Brown 1981, 274). Phrases such as "a deep-seated schizophrenia" (Hederman and Kearney, 94, 1977) "evasiveness" (de Paor 1979, 354), or the more prosaic gap between the "potential and performance of sovereignty" (J. Lee 1989, 361) crop up in contemporary discussions of Irish identity. Such language is readily applicable to the story of industrial development, which was marked by commitments to self-sufficiency, native control, decentralization, and male employment—all poorly fulfilled. However, these critics ignore the role of such compromises and ambiguities in forging consensus in a country riven by civil war and the dislocation consequent on independence, though this was achieved by largely excluding the Protestant/unionist identity.

While the formal political divisions resulting from the civil war survived, by the eve of World War II the wide ideological gulfs that had existed between the two major political parties had virtually disappeared. Both supported wartime neutrality, greater independence from Britain, legislative support for Catholic social teaching

171

and, it would appear, the new-style Irish economy consisting of a protected industrial sector coupled with a dominant cattle-exporting agriculture and subsidized minor agricultural enterprises, closely linked to Britain by trade, banking, and currency.

The basic equilibrium reached by Irish society in 1939 remained intact until the late 1950s when a major economic and psychological crisis forced a reorientation towards a more open economy. The socioeconomic criteria of the thirties—domestic ownership of industry, decentralization of factories, and male employment—also survived into the postwar years. The priority of native industrial ownership, which was always heavily compromised, was partly undermined in 1949 by the establishment of the Industrial Development Authority to promote foreign investment and was ended in 1958 with the easing of the Control of Manufactures Act. Decentralization of industry and male employment remained part of Irish industrial policy until the 1970s when the effects of major urban unemployment and feminism forced retreat on both fronts.

The evolution of industrial policy had long-term consequences, both for the performance of the Irish economy and for the broader shaping of Irish society. Efforts to dismantle the protectionist/ nationalist model failed in the years immediately following World War II because of the strength of the late 1930s accommodation and the absence of major challenge either internal or external. Thus what one writer has termed "our first self definition" was dependent on the acceptance of the 1930s socioeconomic model; its rejection in the fifties and the apparently increased reliance on foreign capital has been regarded as the factor that triggered a modern identity crisis (Fennell 1983, 30, chap. 2). Most of the shortcomings of Irish industry that were revealed in the fifties, such as lack of dynamism and inability to export, were inherent from the beginning.

Despite official rhetoric favoring native industry, a majority of output and employment was probably derived from firms that were dependent on foreign expertise, capital, or trademarks. This dependence may have been inevitable if an industrial structure was to be developed as rapidly as Irish needs dictated; however, the camouflaging of this problem postponed an awareness of the inherent drawbacks. Foreign control meant that decisions such as export expansion frequently lay outside Irish hands and guaranteed that most companies would never compete on the export market. That Irish wages and working conditions equaled or exceeded British levels also militated against international competitiveness.

The long-term efficiency of protected firms was further circumscribed by the dominant attitude of noncompetitiveness. Both Lemass and his officials appear to have sought a situation where output, supplemented perhaps by import quotas, precisely met market demand, and official directives organizing companies into noncompeting specializations were common. The tolerance of noncompetitiveness was increased by the priority given to social criteria such as decentralization, which raised costs and afforded industrialists a potent argument in favor of higher prices and greater protection. This could have been rectified by stronger price regulation, but as much inefficiency stemmed from government action, this would only have exposed the contradictions inherent in official policy.

Alternative policies could have been followed, though options were limited in the difficult economic circumstances of the twenties and thirties. The Cumann na nGaedheal approach of continuity with the policies followed under the Union does not seem a serious alternative unless Irish ambitions to reverse postfamine population decline, end emigration, and increase industrial employment were to be totally abandoned. State intervention has been assumed essential to successful economic transformation in this century (Rueschemeyer and Evans 1985, 45). Government intervention was consequently almost essential. However, it could have followed the lines suggested by Industry and Commerce officials in the twenties. Devaluation of the Irish currency against an over-valued sterling would have reduced deflation with considerable benefit to agriculture while offering a measure of protection to industry. This could have been coupled with selective subsidies for investment and exports, vocational training and export promotion. However, such a program would have entailed major intervention in banking and financial matters, something that even Fianna Fail fought shy of doing.

An alternative scenario would have substituted increased state investment for many of the larger private monopolies or quasi-monopolies such as flour, cement, and the oil refining. This move would have been in keeping with the actions of many other late-industrializing countries, exemplifying Gerschenkron's thesis that the later the industrialization, the greater the need for state involvement (1966, 44). It would have reduced the level of foreign industrial control and might have ultimately led to a more effective Irish managerial class. If combined with restructuring of the banking and financial system, such investment could have been funded by reinvesting money previously invested abroad.

The exploration of such hypothetical scenarios reveals the conservative nature of Irish economic policy, even under Fianna Fail. While its policies resulted in a new economic elite, the existing elite was not attacked, with the temporary exception of the Irish cattle farmer during the economic war. Although there was a widespread if vague desire for industrial development, the combined forces of beer, biscuits, and cattle interests, a British-oriented trading and financial system, and a Catholic, peasant mentality proved formidable obstacles to change. The late nineteenth-century stirring of Irish nationalism through language revival and the adulation of traditional peasant society was explicitly antimodern in its approach and saw a new Ireland as rejecting the materialism of an urban industrialized society. The Cumann na nGaedheal government subscribed to these values by endeavoring to focus Irish economic destiny on agriculture; however, this vision was doomed by postwar deflation and by unfavorable price and cost structures.

International depression and the ending of emigration forced a major rethinking of economic strategy, but the initiative still rested in agrarian hands. It is questionable whether the 1932 self-sufficiency experiment could have been attempted if difficult conditions had not created sufficient agricultural support for protection to remove the implicit farming veto over industrial tariffs that had existed throughout the twenties. The heightened sense of Irish nationalism, the international economic crisis, British protectionism, and the virtual ending of emigration also favored such an experiment, while the conservative tone of the new policies with their emphasis on nationalism and peasant values helped diffuse fears of socialism and modernization. Fianna Fail offered a blueprint for the economic crisis that seemed fully compatible with the maintenance, perhaps even the strengthening, of traditional Irish values.

By the late thirties international collapse had been averted, emigration had resumed, and government programs were not producing the promised revitalization of Irish rural society. Consequently the attack on cattle farming, reflecting a deep-seated antagonism in Irish radical agrarian traditions, was ended, and cattle farmers regained their dominant position, though this time they were harnessed to protected rather than export manufacturers. The 1938 agreement reflected a new alliance of conservative forces in Irish society: owner-occupying farmers, protected manufacturers, and equally protected industrial workers. The social patterns imposed on Irish industrialization by Fianna Fail and the 1938 accommodation ensured that industry would remain a secondary force in the economy with limited capacity for growth and that emigration would persist. A fundamental industrial revolution would have required what Gerschenkron has termed "a New Deal in emotions" (1966, xx, 25). While Fianna Fail attempted a new deal, it was not one conducive to the creation of a modern industrial society.

While the economic program initiated in 1932 involved substantial intervention in the economy, key economic initiatives and profits remained in the hands of private enterprise. Many Irish historians have drawn attention to the innovative nature of Irish semistate bodies such as the Electricity Supply Board (ESB), the Agricultural Credit Company (ACC), and the Industrial Credit Company (ICC). More striking are the relatively small numbers involved and their noncompeting status vis-à-vis private business. Both the ESB and the Irish Sugar Company were set up to avert fears of private monopoly and consequent large profits. The ACC and ICC were structured to avoid impinging directly on the private banking system, while both the Industrial Alcohol Company (Monarchana Alcoil na hEireann Teoranta) and the Turf Development Board (Bord na Mona) were established to achieve social goals that no private company would have tackled. Cumann na nGaedheal hoped that the ACC would be taken over by the cooperative movement, while some elements in Fianna Fail wished to place both the sugar company and the ICC in private hands.

The absence of an ideological role for the state in either Cumann na nGaedheal or Fianna Fail and the legacy of the British civil service tradition are reflected in such attitudes and in the uncertainty about how to run a state company typified by Gordon Campbell and John Leydon, both of whom were exhausted by the trivia of the ESB and the Industrial Alcohol Company. It would have been somewhat surprising if Cumann na nGaedheal had articulated such a role, given its gradual evolution of a conservative economic line; Fianna Fail's ambiguity is more puzzling. The party came into office committed to reducing the burden of government—a promise it singularly failed to keep. Fianna Fail's apparent reluctance to advocate greater government involvement reflects some of the pressures of Irish society. Given the dominance of a Catholic, rural, property-owning population, an active state conjured up fears of socialism and threats to private property. In 1931 De Valera explicitly announced his respect for private property. Socialism and a centralized, bureaucratic state were equally anathema to Catholic social teaching, which preferred a state containing self-contained, largely self-organizing interests (Cahill 1932, 472–73). The Commission on Vocational Organisation criticized the Department of Industry and Commerce on the grounds of excessive regulation, though industrial profits were free from control. Such criticism would have been more vocal and more widely supported if government had been seen to take potentially profitable enterprises from private hands. The CBC Commission attacked state enterprise both for competing with the private sector in potentially profitable areas such as agricultural and industrial credit and for subsidizing nonprofitable projects, denouncing both profitable and unprofitable activities.

The British legacy of a weak state (Skocpol 1985, 3–28; Cronin 1988, 199–231) without a significant tradition of government economic intervention was of crucial importance. The Irish public service inherited the British practice of stringent Treasury spending control coupled with a profound distaste for government involvement in the economy. Such attitudes were poorly suited to Irish needs; in contrast, the Japanese colonial legacy to Taiwan and Korea included an entrepreneurial and interventionist public service ethos (Amsden 1985, 79).

The weak-state model was acceptable to Irish banking and financial interests and to agricultural and industrial exporters, yet it contradicted a deep-seated Irish belief in the efficacy of state action. Consequently it did not meet the expectations of many Irish citizens who, despite being ruled by a weak British state, had developed a strong dependence on government assistance for everything from famine relief to land reform. In 1817 Sir Robert Peel, then chief secretary for Ireland, reviewing the efficacy of his famine relief efforts in the previous season, commented that "the people attributed their relief in a much greater degree to the intervention of the Government than they ought to have done" (quoted in Jenkins 1987, 132). Britain pandered to such dependence by doling out lollipops in the form of roads, drainage schemes, fishery development, or light railways without evolving any clear economic role for the state beyond the vague doctrine that Ireland, or at least rural Ireland, was different from England.

The new state inherited the contradictory strains of widespread popular expectations of state assistance and a civil service to whom this was anathema. One consequence of such contradictions was to restrict the state to quasi-social or philanthropic duties that had been deemed acceptable under the Union, as opposed to a more positive entrepreneurial function. The allocation of industrial alcohol factories, which was primarily determined by social rather than economic criteria, is an example of government intervention in the direct tradition of nineteenth-century spending on piers and light railways.

The division of opinion on the role of the state is evident at both civil service and governmental levels. While the Department of Finance upheld the Treasury attitude, Industry and Commerce appears to have been more sympathetic towards government intervention. However, even within Industry and Commerce conflicting attitudes emerge. Opinions also varied within the cabinet, though the positions of key individuals often lacked consistency. Lemass favored a strongly directive industrial policy with mandatory licensing and control over all firms, both native and foreign, and over exports and imports, measures that his colleagues were not prepared to accept. At the same time he seems to have been prepared to concede considerable monopoly powers to foreign industrial interests, as in the case of cement. Colleagues who opposed some of Lemass's more authoritarian proposals seem on occasion to have sought similar powers for their pet projects such as the development of Gaeltacht industry.

Most attitudes were pragmatic responses to departmental needs or to individual political or constituency wishes, rather than the consequence of any clearly articulated position on the role of the state. Ministers and officials grappling with such issues received little guidance from the economics profession, which appears to have adopted a position of universal opposition to any minor divergence from the canons of free trade and neoclassical economics. While John Maynard Keynes (1933) saw some merits in the Irish espousal of protection, native economists did not. George O'Brien, whose economic histories constituted a strong argument in favor of government intervention and protection in the past was either unable or unwilling to apply these arguments to contemporary issues. The upshot was a program of state involvement that was largely ad hoc and occasionally contradictory and that evolved without any clear ideological or intellectual rationale.

One major legacy of the thirties was the institutionalization of an Irish dependence on the state, and on politicians, for economic benefits. This reliance had evolved during the nineteenth century under British rule, and although Cumann na nGaedheal appears to have attempted to break it, Fianna Fail policies brought a considerable extension. Decisions on tariffs or quotas, allocations of quotas and duty-free import licenses, the location of factories, and numerous other matters became largely discretionary decisions determined by ministers and officials. In consequence, lobbying and deputations were seen as essential to attract an industry to a particular town or to the profitability of a new concern. Farm incomes came to depend on the outcome of Anglo-Irish trade talks or on price and subsidy levels set by the state.

Some increase in dependence on the state was inevitable given the decision to expand protection. However, it could have been reduced by standardizing levels of assistance, by making them publicly known, and by refraining from government involvement in trivial decisions. Tariff levels could have been set automatically at two or three different rates instead of being individually negotiated. Instead of awarding discretionary duty-free import licenses to favored manufacturers, licenses for the import of machinery could have been automatically granted, or machinery could have been left free of tariffs. Decisions on location could have been left to industrialists, with differential tariff rates available as a regional incentive. Such options would have reduced the cost of government without loss of efficiency, though they might have reduced the potential to influence industry for social ends and would have deprived the government party of potentially beneficial political support.

While industry became heavily dependent on government for profitability and often for survival, the government proved either unable or unwilling to use its powers to bring about a more efficient industrial sector. In the 1920s McElligott of the Department of Finance argued against protection on the grounds that once granted it would prove difficult to withdraw (Fanning 1978, 203–4), a concern that proved all too correct in the Irish case. Officials were aware of the shortcomings of protected firms but appear powerless to remedy them, perhaps because a government could not be seen to directly bring about the collapse of a particular firm.

Whether efficiency could have been achieved by making the industrial sector—both employers and employees—responsible for itself by establishing consultative, corporate institutions remains problematical. While Katzenstein (1985) has lauded the recent economic performance of small European democratic states that have a high level of government assistance and strong corporate institutions, he emphasizes that the economies in question are heavily exposed to international competition and sees this as essential to their efficiency. The Irish economy of the thirties lacked this vital ingredient. In addition the corporatist institutions of the continental economies had evolved over a long period. Ireland was in the process of both a political revolution and a revolution in elites, from a nineteenth century where these were dominated by the Anglo-Irish and primarily oriented towards links with Britain to a new, Irish-centered, nationalist elite. Such transitions among employer and worker organizations and the absence of corporatist traditions made the emergence of mediating institutions unlikely even had the political will to favor them existed.

Ultimately the power of government was mediated not by formal institutions, but by informal links between government and key individuals—a process made easier by Ireland's small size. Business figures such as Arthur Cox or Vincent Crowley retained close contact with the Industrial Credit Company's J. J. Beddy—a transitional figure between the state and private sectors—and Sean Lemass; similar relations may have existed with trade unionists.

The most fundamental question to be faced about Irish industrial policy concerns the economic ambitions of both governments and people. Criticisms concerning the efficiency of new industries and the adequacy of the growth in employment and output presuppose a commitment to modern targets of economic growth that cannot be assumed. The Irish desire for self-sufficiency and industrialization under native control without the incursion of the modern world set targets not capable of being judged by conventional criteria such as growth of GNP. There is little doubt that the unduly ambitious aims of Fianna Fail and of earlier generations of nationalists were not met: emigration did not end; self-sufficiency was not achieved; the numbers living on the land declined; dependence on Britain for exports and imports remained strong; Dublin grew rapidly despite official wishes to the contrary. However, the country achieved the first sustained growth in industrial employment for a century at a rate not yet surpassed, and while growth of GNP was lower than the British rate, the economic crisis of the thirties was significantly less acute than in most European countries, perhaps because of the structure of the Irish economy. Hunger marches and social unrest were avoided, and the poor and unemployed were better cared for than in previous decades. Increased taxes on income and high protective duties meant a transfer of resources from sectors such as public service, transport, trade, retailing, and finance, which had escaped the worst effects of free trade, to welfare recipients and industrial workers.

The emergence of a new economic elite dependent on government helped redress the largely unionist sympathies of the dominant Irish business establishment in 1922 and brought an increase in Irish industrial expertise. The failure of Craig Gardner, Dublin's largest accountancy firm, to gain government business or significant work from new protected companies reflects the shift in the political and religious composition of the Irish business elite (Farmar 1988, 133–34). While the attempted economic break with Britain in 1932 was an extreme move of doubtful benefit, it ended any tendency to view the Irish economy in terms of union with Britain. Even those who had yearned to return to the pre-1922 patterns were grateful for the new political and economic relationship as defined by the 1938 agreement.

For men and women forced to emigrate from Ireland in these years, for families condemned to survive on inadequately small landholdings unable to find alternative employment, for young people who were incapable of marrying in Ireland because of inadequate employment and income, the failure of government policies in both the twenties and thirties is not in doubt. However, as we have seen, industrialization was viewed with considerable ambivalence by many elements in Irish society. Opposition criticism of the "new plutocracy" of industrialists that had emerged and De Valera's lament in 1939 over his failure to prevent the flight from the land and his speculation whether the spread of radio might have given country people "ideas about town life" (PDDE 7 July 1939) suggest that even the relatively modest social changes of the thirties aroused fears that the fabric of Irish society was threatened.

More rapid or more extensive industrialization would have aroused considerably greater tensions, with the loss of rural dominance and the threat of changes in Irish family patterns and political attitudes. Irish society was still recovering from the stress of the civil war, striving to establish itself as an independent state. In the 1920s Ireland fastened on Catholicism and the Irish language to define the country's separate identity (O'Callaghan 1984, 226–45). Fianna Fail successfully extended this identity into the economic sphere with its commitment, however compromised, to native control, decentralized industry, and women staying in the home. The political scientist Karl Deutsch wrote of the need to build up national strength and of integration:

> On the first "tack" when power must be organized, or a community must be built, the prime need is for cohesion, for the close complementarity of parts to force them into one dependable whole. Here we meet the builders of states and nations, the princes, the revolutionists, or the nationalistic spokesmen, as the great simplifiers, the destroyers of diversity and localism on the one hand, and at the same time the great "narrowers", as the eliminators of foreign influences, as the relative isolators of their developing communities from much of the rest of the world. Only the most carefully screened and selected influences from the outside world are henceforth to be admitted to the budding nation, and usually they are to be confined to narrowly technical, economic or scientific matters, in regard to which the foreigners are to be "over-taken and surpassed" without admitting any broader foreign values, habits, or culture patterns to consideration. (1966, 83)

If the rapid economic growth of the sixties and the growing materialism, urbanism, and internationalism led to an apparent identity crisis in recent decades, such strains would have been even greater on a new and insecure nation. Given the strong wish for stability it can be argued that the modest and perhaps slightly confused economic achievements of the twenties and thirties met the dominant needs of Irish society. That these needs also dictated the emigration of a significant proportion of the youth of Ireland merely reflects a fundamental continuity with postfamine decades under the Union.

Bibliography
Index

# Bibliography

*Manuscript Sources*

Bank of Ireland Archives, Dublin.
    Irish Banks Standing Committee. Minutes.
    Geoffrey Crowther. Memorandum on credit policy. 1932.
    Secretary's file. Clay to Lord Glenavy, 28 Mar. 1934.
Confederation of Irish Industry, Federation House, Dublin.
    Federation of Irish Manufacturers (FIM). Minutes; annual report.
    Federation of Saorstat Industries.
    Federation of Irish Industries (FII). Minutes; annual reports.
Department of Finance.[1]
    Finance series (F).
    Supply series (S).
Department of Industry and Commerce.
    Control of Manufactures Act temporary file.
    Industries files: Inds. series (Inds.); Inds. A series (Inds. A); Inds. B series
        (Inds. B).
    Trade and Industries Division (TID).
    Trade, Industries, and Mining Division (TIM).
    Trade Facilities Act I/58 I/D.
Dublin Municipal Archives, City Hall, Dublin.
    B1/ Records of Stokes and Kelly, Bruce, Symes and Wilson, stockbrokers,
        24 Anglesea Street, Dublin.

---

1. The records of both the Department of Finance and the Department of Industry and Commerce have now been transferred to the National Archives in Dublin.

Dublin Stock Exchange.
   Stock market listings, 1924–1939.
Industrial Credit Company (ICC), Harcourt Street, Dublin 2.
   Annual reports; minutes of annual general meetings.
National Library of Ireland.
   NLI Brennan Papers (B Papers), 26290, 26290A.
   NLI Frank Gallagher Papers, MS 18339.
   NLI Commission on Vocational Organisation (CVO), minutes, NLI
      MSS 932–51.
   NLI Dublin Industrial Development Association (DIDA), minutes and
      reports. NLI MS 16242.
   NLI National Agricultural and Industrial Development Association
      (NAIDA) minutes and reports NLI MSS 16243–44.
Public Record Office, London.
   Board of Trade (BT) BT 11 series.
   Cabinet Papers. Cab. 27 series; cabinet committees.
   Treasury Papers. T160 series (T).
National Archives, Dublin.
   Cabinet Conclusions. C series.
   Cabinet Papers. S series.
   G.C. series 1938.
University College Dublin Archives.
   Blythe Papers.
   McGilligan Papers (McG Papers).
   Mulcahy Papers.

*Printed Works*

IRISH GOVERNMENT PUBLICATIONS

Banking Commission. 1926. Second, third, and fourth interim reports.
   R 33/2.
————. 1927. Final Report. R 33/3.
*Census of Population.* 1926, 1936.
*Census of Production.* 1926, 1929, 1931, 1936, 1937, 1938.
Commission on Vocational Organisation. 1943. Report. P6743 (1944). R 77.
Companies Office. Annual Reports, 1924/1940.
Currency, Banking, and Credit Commission of Inquiry. 1938. Report. R38.
Dail Eireann. 1923. Commission on Industrial Resources.
————. 1923. Fiscal Inquiry Committee Reports. R20.
————. 1924. Commission on Agriculture Interim Report. R25.

————. 1924. Commission on Agriculture Final Report. R25.

————. 1926. Banking and Currency First Interim Report. R33/1.

Economic Committee (1928). 1929. First and second interim reports. R42.

Flour and Bread Commission of Inquiry. Report. 1951. R81.

Flour Milling Industry. Report of the survey team established by the Minister for Agriculture. 1965. A53/5.

Grain Inquiry Tribunal Report. 1931. R44.

Minister of Agriculture. 1932–1933 to 1939–1940. reports.

Tariff Commission. 1926. R 36/2. Application for a Tariff on Margarine.

————. 1927. R 36/5. Application for a Tariff on Down Quilts.

————. 1927. R 36/1. Application for a Tariff on Rosaries.

————. 1927. R 36/4. Application for a Tariff on Woollens.

————. 1928. R 36/3. Application for a Tariff on Flour.

————. 1929. R 36/44. Report no. 4 supplementary.

————. 1929. R 36/6. Application for a Tariff on Fish Barrels.

————. 1930. R 36/13. Application for a Tariff on Linen Piece Goods.

————. 1930. R 36/8. Application for a Tariff on Motor Vehicles.

————. 1930. R 36/7. Application for a Tariff on Packing and Papers.

————. 1931. R 36/9. Application for a Tariff on Butter.

————. 1931. R 36/11. Application for a Tariff on Leather.

————. 1931. R 36/12. Application for a Tariff on Oats.

————. 1931. R 36/10. Application for a Tariff on Woollens and Worsted, Modification.

————. 1932. R 36/14. Application for a Tariff on Bacon, Hams.

————. 1934. R 36/15. Application for a Tariff on Books of Prayer.

DEBATES

Published Debates Dail Eireann (PDDE)

Published Debates Seanad Eireann (PDSE)

NEWSPAPERS AND PERIODICALS

*The Economist*

*Irish Industrial Yearbook*

*Irish Industry*

*Irish Times*

*Irish Trade Journal*

BRITISH GOVERNMENT PUBLICATION

Finance and Industry Committee. 1931. Cmd 3897.

BOOKS, ARTICLES, THESES

Aitken, Hugh, ed. 1959. "Defensive Expansionism: The State and Economic Growth in Canada." In *The State and Economic Growth,* ed. H. Aitken, 79–114. New York: Social Science Research Council.

———. 1959. *The State and Economic Growth.* New York: Social Science Research Council.

Aldcroft, D. H., and H. W. Richardson. 1969. *The British Economy, 1870–1919.* London: Macmillan.

Amsden, Alice. 1985. "The State and Taiwan's Economic Development." In *Bringing the State Back In,* ed. P. Evans, D. Rueschemeyer, and T. Skocpol, 44–77. New York: Cambridge Univ. Press.

Andrews, C. S. 1982. *Man of No Property.* Dublin: Mercier.

Barrington, Ruth. 1987. *Health, Medicine, and Politics in Ireland, 1900–1970.* Dublin: Institute of Public Administration.

Berger, Suzanne. 1972. *Peasants Against Politics.* Cambridge, Mass.: Harvard Univ. Press.

Broadberry, S. N. 1984. "The North European Depression of the 1920s." *Scandinavian Economic History Review* 32, no. 3: 159–67.

Brown, Jonathan. 1987. *Agriculture in England: A Survey of Farming, 1870–1945.* Manchester: Manchester Univ. Press.

Brown, Terence. 1981. *Ireland: A Social and Cultural History, 1922–79.* London: Fontana.

Butlin, Noel G. 1959. "Colonial Socialism in Australia, 1860–1900." In *The State and Economic Growth,* ed. H. Aitken, 26–78. New York: Social Science Research Council.

Cahill, Edward. 1932. *The Framework of a Christian State.* Dublin: M. H. Gill.

Canning, P. 1987. *British Policy towards Ireland, 1921–41.* Oxford: Oxford Univ. Press.

Capie, Forrest. 1983. *Depression and Protectionism: Britain between the Wars.* London: Allen and Unwin.

Cipolla, Carlo, ed. 1976. *Fontana Economic History of Europe.* Vol. 6, *Contemporary Economies.* Parts 1 and 2. London: Fontana.

Conniffe, Denis, and Kieran A. Kennedy. 1984. *Employment and Unemployment Policy for Ireland.* Dublin: Economic and Social Research Institute.

Connolly, James. 1973. *Labour in Irish History.* Dublin: New Books.

Conybeare, A. C. 1983. "Tariff Protection in Developed and Developing Countries: A Cross-Sectional and Longitudinal Analysis." *International Organization* 37:441–68.

Coyne, W. P., ed. 1902. *Ireland: Industrial and Agricultural.* Dublin: Department of Agriculture and Technical Instruction.

Cronin, James E. 1988. "The British State and the Structure of Political Opportunity." *Journal of British Studies* (July) 27:199–231.

Crotty, R. 1966. *Irish Agricultural Production: Its Volume and Structure.* Cork: Cork Univ. Press.

Cullen, L. M. 1968. *Anglo-Irish Trade, 1600–1800.* Manchester: Manchester Univ. Press.

———. 1969. "Irish Economic History: Fact and Myth." In *The Formation of the Irish Economy,* ed. L. M. Cullen. Cork: Mercier.

———. 1983. *Princes and Pirates. The Dublin Chamber of Commerce, 1783–1983.* Dublin: Dublin Chamber of Commerce.

Curtis, Maurice. 1981. "Trade Union Activity in the Boot and Shoe Industry in Ireland, 1932–38." M. A. thesis, Univ. College Dublin.

Daly, Mary E. 1978. "Women, Work, and Trade Unionism." In *Women in Irish Society,* ed. Margaret MacCurtain and Donncha O'Corrain, 71–81. Dublin: Arlen House.

———. 1984a. "Government Finance for Industry in the Irish Free State: The Trade Loans (Guarantee) Acts." *Irish Economic and Social History* 11:73–93.

———. 1984b. "An Irish-Ireland for Business? The Control of Manufactures Acts, 1932 and 1934." *Irish Historical Studies* 24, no. 94 (Nov.):246–72.

———. 1988. "The Employment Gains from Industrial Protection in the Irish Free State during the 1930s: A Note." *Irish Economic and Social History,* 15:71–75.

Davis, Richard. 1974. *Arthur Griffith and Non-Violent Sinn Fein.* Dublin: Anvil.

———. 1989. *The Young Ireland Movement.* Dublin: Gill and Macmillan.

de Paor, Liam. 1979. "Ireland's Identities." *Crane Bag* 3, no. 1: 354–61.

Deutsch, Karl W. 1966. *Nationalism and Social Communication. An Inquiry into the Foundation of Nationality.* Cambridge, Mass.: MIT Press.

Drummond, Ian M. 1974. *Imperial Economic Policy, 1917–39. Studies in Expansion and Protection.* London: Allen and Unwin.

Evans, Peter, Dietrich Rueschemeyer, and Theda Skocpol, eds. 1985. *Bringing the State Back In.* Cambridge Univ. Press.

Fanning, Ronan. 1978. *The Irish Department of Finance, 1922–58.* Dublin: Institue of Public Administration.

———. 1983. *Independent Ireland.* Dublin: Helicon.

Farmar, Tony. 1988. *A History of Craig Gardner and Co.: The First Hundred Years.* Dublin: Gill and Macmillan.

Farrell, Brian. 1983. *Sean Lemass.* Dublin: Gill and Macmillan.

Fennell, Desmond. 1983. *The State of the Nation. Ireland since the Sixties.* Dublin: Ward River.

Ferguson, R. C. 1944. "Industrial Policy." In *Public Administration in Ireland,* ed. F. C. King, 78–121. Vol. 1. Dublin: Parkside.

Fitzgerald, Garret. 1959. "Mr. Whitaker and Industry." *Studies* 48:138–50.

Foster, Roy. 1988. *Modern Ireland, 1600–1972.* London: Allen Lane.

Fox, Alan, 1958. *A History of the National Union of Boot and Shoe Operatives, 1874–1957.* Oxford: Basil Blackwell.

Garvin, Tom. 1987. *Nationalist Revolutionaries in Ireland 1858–1928.* Oxford: Clarendon.

Gaughan, Anthony. 1980. *Thomas Johnson, 1872–1963.* Dublin: Kingdom Books.

Gerschenkron, Alexander. 1962. *Economic Backwardness in Historical Perspective.* Cambridge, Mass.: Harvard Univ. Press.

Gourevitch, Peter Alexis. 1984. "Breaking with Orthodoxy: The Politics of Economic Policy Responses to the Depression of the 1930s." *International Organization* 38:95–129.

————. 1987. *Politics in Hard Times.* Cornell Univ. Press.

Hall F. G. 1946. *The Bank of Ireland, 1783–1946.* Dublin: Hodges Figgis.

Hancock, W. K. 1937. *Survey of British Commonwealth Affairs:* Vol. 1. *Problems of Nationality, 1918–1936.* Oxford: Oxford Univ. Press.

Hardach, Karl. 1976. "Germany." In *Fontana Economic History of Europe,* ed. C. Cipolla. Vol. 6, *Contemporary Economies.* Part 1, 180–265. London: Fontana.

Hederman, Mark Patrick, and Richard Kearney, eds. 1977. "A Sense of Nation." *Crane Bag* 1, no. 2.

Hoppen, K. Theodore. 1984. *Elections, Politics, and Society in Ireland, 1832–1885.* Oxford: Oxford Univ. Press.

Irish Trade Union Congress. 1914–1942. Reports.

Irish Transport and General Workers Union. 1919–1939. Annual Reports.

Jacobsen, D. S. 1977. "The Political Economy of Industrial Location: The Ford Motor Company at Cork, 1912–26." *Irish Economic and Social History* 4:36–55.

Jenkins, Brian. 1987. *Era of Emancipation. British Government of Ireland, 1812–30.* Montreal: McGill Univ. Press.

Johansen, Hans Christian. 1987. *The Danish Economy in the Twentieth Century.* London: Routledge.

Johnson, David. 1985. *The Interwar Eonomy in Ireland.* Studies in Irish Economic and Social History no. 4. Dublin: Economic & Social History Society of Ireland.

————. 1988. "Reply." *Irish Economic and Social History* 15:76–80.

Jones, Edgar. 1986. "Steel and Engineering Overseas: Guest, Keen, and Nettlefold's Multinational Growth, 1918–65." In *British Multinationals: Origins, Management, and Performance,* ed. G. Jones. London: Aldershot Gower.

Jones, Geoffrey, ed. 1986. *British Multinationals: Origins, Management, and Performance.* London:

Jones, Mary. 1988. *These Obstreperous Lassies: A History of the Irish Women Workers' Union.* Dublin: Gill and Macmillan.

Jorberg, Lennart, and Olle Krantz. 1976. "Scandinavia, 1914–70." In *Fontana Economic History of Europe,* ed. C. Cipolla. Vol. 6, *Contemporary Economies.* Part 2, 377–459. London: Fontana.

Kane, Robert. 1844. *Industrial Resources of Ireland.* Dublin: Hodges and Smith.

Katzenstein, Peter J. 1985. *Small States in World Markets. Industrial Policy in Europe.* Ithaca, N.Y.: Cornell Univ. Press.

Kennedy, Kieran A. 1971. *Productivity and Industrial Growth. The Irish Experience.* Oxford: Oxford Univ. Press.

Kennedy, Kieran A., Thomas Giblin, and Deirdre McHugh. 1988. *The Economic Development of Ireland in the Twentieth Century.* London: Routledge.

Keogh, Dermot. 1983. "De Valera, the Catholic Church, and the 'Red Scare,' 1931–32" In *De Valera and His Times,* ed. J. P. O'Carroll and J. A. Murphy, 134–59. Cork: Cork Univ. Press.

Kerwin, Robert W. 1959. "Etatism in Turkey, 1933–52." In *The State and Economic Growth,* ed. H. Aitken, 255–86. New York: Social Science Research Council.

Keynes, J. M. 1933. "National Self-Sufficiency." *Studies* 22: 177–93.

Lee, C. H. 1969. "The Effects of the Depression on Primary Producing Countries." *Journal of Contemporary History* 4, no. 4:139–56.

Lee, Joseph. 1979. "Aspects of Corporatist Thought in Ireland: The Commission on Vocational Organisation, 1939–43." In *Studies in Irish History Presented to R. Dudley Edwards,* ed. A. Cosgrove and D. McCartney, 324–46. Dublin: Univ. College Dublin.

————. 1989. *Ireland, 1912–1985. Politics and Society.* Cambridge: Cambridge Univ. Press.

Lowe, Marvin E. 1942. *The British Tariff Movement.* Washington, D. C.: American Council on Public Affairs.

Lyons, F. S. L. 1971. *Ireland Since the Famine.* London: Weidenfeld and Nicolson.

————. 1977. *Parnell.* London:

McAleese, Dermot. 1971. *Effective Tariffs and the Structure of Industrial Protection in Ireland.* ESRI paper no. 62. (June).

McCarthy, Charles. 1977. *Trade Unions in Ireland, 1894–1960.* Dublin: Institute of Public Administration.

McDonagh, Oliver. 1977. *Ireland: the Union and its Aftermath.* London: Allen and Unwin.

McGuire, E. B. 1938. *The British Tariff System.* London: Methuen.

McMahon, Deirdre. 1984. *Republicans and Imperialists. Anglo-Irish Relations in the 1930s.* New Haven: Yale Univ. Press.

Manning, Maurice, and Moore McDowell. 1984. *Electricity Supply in Ireland. The History of the ESB.* Dublin: Gill and Macmillan.

Mansergh, Nicholas. 1965. *The Irish Question, 1840–1921.* London: Allen and Unwin.

Maynooth Union. 1909. *Records of the Maynooth Union.* Dublin: Browne and Nolan.

———. 1914. *Records of the Maynooth Union, 1913–14.* Dublin: Browne and Nolan.

Meenan, James. 1970. *The Irish Economy since 1922.* Liverpool: Liverpool Univ. Press.

———. 1980. *George O'Brien, a Biographical memoir.* Dublin: Gill and Macmillan.

Moss, W. 1933. *Political Parties in the Irish Free State.* New York: Columbia Univ. Press.

Moynihan, M. 1975. *Currency and Central Banking in Ireland, 1922–1960.* Dublin: Gill and Macmillan.

———. ed. 1980. *Speeches and Statements by Eamon de Valera, 1917–73.* Dublin: Gill and Macmillan.

Murray, A. 1903. *The Commercial Relations between Great Britain and Ireland.* London: London School of Economics and Political Science.

Neary, J. Peter, and Cormac O'Grada. 1986. *Protection, Economic War, and Structural Change: The 1930s in Ireland.* U.C.D. Centre for Economic Research working paper no. 40.

O'Brien, George. 1920. "Historical Introduction." In *Modern Irish Trade and Industry,* by E. J. Riordan. London: Methuen.

O'Callaghan, Margaret. 1984. "Language, Nationality, and Cultural Identity in the Irish Free State, 1922–7: The *Irish Statesman* and *Catholic Bulletin* Reappraised." *Irish Historical Studies* 24, no. 94: 226–45.

O'Carroll, J. P., and John A. Murphy, eds. 1983. *De Valera and His Times.* Cork: Cork Univ. Press.

O'Connor, R., and C. Guiomard. 1985. "Agricultural Output in the Irish Free State Area before and after Independence." *Irish Economic and Social History* 12:89–97.

O'Crualaoich, Gearoid. 1983. "The Primacy of Form: A 'Folk Ideology' in De Valera's Politics." In *De Valera and His Times,* ed. J. P. O'Carroll and J. A. Murphy, 47–61. Cork: Cork Univ. Press.

O'Hagan, John W. 1980. "An Analysis of the Relative Size of the Government Sector: Ireland, 1926–52." *Economic and Social Review* 12, no. 1 (Oct.):17–36.

O'Halloran, Clare. 1987. *Partition and the Limits of Irish Nationalism.* Dublin: Gill and Macmillan.

Olleranshaw, Philip. 1988. "Aspects of Bank Lending in Post-Famine Ireland. In *Economy and Society in Scotland and Ireland, 1500–1939,* ed. R. Mitchison and P. Roebuck. Edinburgh: John Donald.

Olson, Mancur. 1976. *The Rise and Fall of Nations.* New Haven: Yale Univ. Press.

O'Sullivan, Donal. 1940. *The Irish Free State and Its Senate.* London: Faber.

Plummer, Alfred. 1937. *New British Industries in the Twentieth Century.* London: Pitman and Sons.

Plunkett, Horace. 1905. *Ireland in the New Century.* 3rd. ed. London: John Murray.

Press, J. P. 1986. "Protectionism and the Irish Footwear Industry, 1932–39." *Irish Economic and Social History* 13:74–89.

Recess Committee. 1896. *Report on the Establishment of a Department of Agriculture and Industries for Ireland.* Dublin: Browne and Nolan.

Ricossa, Sergio. 1976. "Italy." In *Fontana Economic History of Europe,* ed. C. Cipolla. Vol. 6, *Contemporary Economies.* Part 1, 266–322. London: Fontana.

Riordan, E. J. 1920. *Modern Irish Trade and Industry.* London: Methuen.

Rueschemeyer, Dietrich, and Peter Evans. 1985. "The State and Economic Transformation." In *Bringing the State Back In,* ed. P. Evans, D. Rueschemeyer, and T. Skocpol, 78–106. New York: Cambridge Univ. Press.

Rumpf, E., and A. C. Hepburn. 1977. *Nationalism and Socialism in Twentieth Century Ireland.* Liverpool: Liverpool Univ. Press.

Ryan, W. J. L. 1948–1949. "Measurement of Tariff Levels in Ireland for 1931, 1936, 1938." *Statistical and Social Inquiry Society Journal* 18: 109–32.

———. 1949. "The Nature and Effects of Protective Policy in Ireland, 1932–39." Ph.D. diss., Dublin Univ.

Sacks, Paul. 1976. The *Donegal Mafia.* New Haven: Yale Univ. Press.

Sarti, Roland. 1971. *Fascism and the Industrial Leadership in Italy, 1919–40.* Berkeley: Univ. of California Press.

Skinner, Liam C. 1946. *Politicians by Accident.* Dublin: Metropolitan.

Skocpol, Theda. 1985. "Bringing the State Back In: Current Research." In *Bringing the State Back In,* ed. P. Evans, D. Rueschemeyer, and T. Skocpol, 3–43. New York: Cambridge Univ. Press.

Spuler, Nicholas. 1959. "The Role of the State in Economic Growth in Eastern Europe since 1860." In *The State and Economic Growth,* ed. H. Aitken, 209–54. New York:

Thomas, W. A. 1986. *The Stock Exchanges of Ireland.* Liverpool: Liverpool Univ. Press.

Wallace, Lillian Parker. 1966. *Leo III and the Rise of Socialism.* Durham, N.C.: Duke Univ. Press.

Walsh, J. J. 1944. *Recollections of a Rebel.* Tralee, County Kerry: Anvil.

Whetham, Edith H. 1976. *Beef, Cattle, and Sheep, 1910–1940.* Cambridge: Cambridge Univ. Press.

———. 1978. *The Agrarian History of England and Wales.* Vol. 8, *1914–39.* Cambridge: Cambridge Univ. Press.

Wiener, Martin J. 1981. *English Culture and the Decline of the Industrial Spirit, 1850–1980.* Cambridge: Cambridge Univ. Press.

# Index

**Industrial Development and Irish National Identity, 1922–1939**
was composed in 12 on 13 Garamond #3 on a Linotronic 300
by Partners Composition;
printed by sheet-fed offset on 50-pound, acid-free Natural Hi Bulk
and Smyth-sewn and bound over binder's boards in Holliston Roxite B
with dust jackets printed in 2 colors
by Braun-Brumfield, Inc.;
published in the United States
by Syracuse University Press
Syracuse, New York 13244-5160;
and published in Ireland
by Gill and Macmillan, Publishers.